Woman at Point Zero

Woman at Point Zero

Nawal El Saadawi

Translated by Sherif Hetata

Zed Books Ltd
London and New York

Woman at Point Zero was originally published in Arabic.
It was first published in English by Zed Books Ltd,
7 Cynthia Street, London N1 9JF, UK and Room 400,
175 Fifth Avenue, New York, NY 10010, USA, in 1983.

www.zedbooks.co.uk

Thirteenth impression, 2004

Cover designed by Andrew Corbett
Cover illustration by Phyllis Mahon
Printed and bound in the United Kingdom
by Cox & Wyman Ltd, Reading, Berkshire

Distributed in the USA exclusively by Palgrave Macmillan, a division
of St Martin's Press, LLC, 175 Fifth Avenue, New York, NY 10010.

A catalogue record for this book is
available from the British Library.

ISBN 0 86232 110 7 Pb

Author's Preface

I wrote this novel after an encounter between me and a woman in Qanatir Prison. A few months before, I had started research on neurosis in Egyptian women, and was able to concentrate most of my time on this work as I was then without a job. At the end of 1972 the Minister of Health had removed from me my functions as Director of Health Education and Editor-in-Chief of the magazine *Health*. This was one more consequence of the path I had chosen as a feminist author and novelist whose views were viewed unfavourably by the authorities.

However, this situation gave me more time to think, to write, to research, and to deal with the consultations which I conducted with women who came to see me. The year 1973 saw a new stage of my life; it also witnessed the birth of my novel *Firdaus*, or *Woman at Point Zero*.

The idea for my research in fact arose as a result of the women who sought my advice and help to deal with situations which had led to a greater or lesser degree of "mental affliction". I decided to choose a limited number of cases from amongst women suffering from neurosis, and this entailed regular visits to a number of hospitals and outpatient clinics.

The idea of "prison" had always exercised a special attraction for me. I often wondered what prison life was like, especially for women. Perhaps this was because I lived in a country where many prominent intellectuals around me had spent various periods of time in prison for "political offences". My husband had been imprisoned for 13 years as a "political detainee". So that when one day I happened to meet one of the doctors from the Women's Prison in Qanatir I was irresistibly drawn to exchange ideas with him; whenever we met we would stop and talk. He told me many things about the women prisoners gaoled for different offences, and especially about those who suffered degrees of neurosis, and who attended the weekly mental clinic of the Qanatir Prison Hospital.

I became more and more interested, and slowly the idea of visiting the prison to see the women there grew on me. The only time I had seen inside a prison was in "political films", but now I had the opportunity to visit a real one. The idea grew even more compelling when my friend the prison doctor began to tell me, at length, about a woman who had killed a man and was under sentence of death by hanging. I had never seen a woman who had killed.

The prison doctor said he would take me to see her, and show me other women prisoners who suffered from mental afflictions. Through him I was enabled to obtain a special permit to visit Qanatir Prison as a psychiatrist and to examine the women. He became so interested in what I planned to undertake that he accompanied me as far as the prison and showed me around once we were inside.

The instant I stepped through the prison gates I was overcome by sudden gloom at the sight of the sullen buildings, the iron-barred windows and the overall harshness of the surroundings. A shiver went through my body. Little did I know that one day I would step through the same gates, not as a psychiatrist, but as a prisoner arrested with 1,035 others under the decree issued by Sadat on 5 September 1981. On that particular morning in the autumn of 1974, however, the possibility of being confined behind the high, bare, yellowish walls never occurred to me. As I crossed the inner court-yards I could glimpse the faces of the women, lurking behind the iron bars like animals, their white or brown fingers twisted around the black metal.

Firdaus at first refused to receive me in her cell, but later she agreed to meet me. Little by little she was brought to tell me her story, the whole story of her life. It was a terrible yet wonderful story. As she unfolded her life before me, as I learnt more and more about her. I developed a feeling and admiration for this woman who seemed to me so exceptional in the world of women to which I was accustomed. So later, the day came when I began to think of writing the novel which came to be known as *Woman at Point Zero* or *Firdaus*.

But for the time being I found myself occupied with the many women whom my doctor friend showed me in the cells and in the mental clinic for they were to constitute a part of the 20 in-depth case studies included in my research, the results of which were published in 1976, under the title *Women and Neurosis in Egypt*.

Firdaus, however, remained a woman apart. She stood out amongst the others, vibrated within me, or sometimes lay quiet, until the day when I put her down in ink on paper and gave her life after she had died. For, at the end of 1974, Firdaus was executed, and I never saw her again. And yet somehow she was always before my eyes. I could see her in front of me, trace the lines of her forehead, her lips, her eyes, watch her as she moved with pride. When, in autumn 1981, it was my turn to be confined behind bars, I would watch the other women prisoners as they moved through the inner courtyard, as though looking for her, trying to glimpse her head which she always held so high, the calm movements of her hands, or the stern look of her brown eyes. I could not bring myself to believe that she had really died.

During the three months I spent in gaol I met a number of women who were accused of having killed a man, some of whom reminded me of Firdaus; yet none of them was like her. She remained unique. Not only her features, her carriage, her courage, or the way she was wont to look at me from the depths of her eyes, distinguished her from other women, but her absolute refusal to live, her absolute fearlessness of death.

Firdaus is the story of a woman driven by despair to the darkest of ends. This woman, despite her misery and despair, evoked in all those who, like me, witnessed the final moments of life, a need to challenge and to overcome those forces that deprive human beings of their right to live, to love and to real freedom.

Nawal El Saadawi
Cairo, September 1983

This is the story of a real woman. I met her in the Qanatir Prison a few years ago. I was doing research on the personalities of a group of women prisoners and detainees convicted or accused of various offences.

The prison doctor told me that this woman had been sentenced to death for killing a man. Yet she was not like the other female murderers held in the prison.

'You will never meet anyone like her in or out of prison. She refuses all visitors, and won't speak to anyone. She usually leaves her food untouched, and remains wide awake until dawn. Sometimes the prison warder observes her as she sits staring vacantly into space for hours. One day she asked for pen and paper, then spent hours hunched over them without moving. The warder could not tell whether she was writing a letter or something else. Perhaps she was not writing anything at all.'

I asked the prison doctor, 'Will she see me?'

'I shall try to persuade her to speak to you for a while,' he said. 'She might agree if I explain you are a psychiatrist, and not one of the Public Prosecutor's assistants. She refuses to answer my questions. She even refused to sign an appeal to the President so that her sentence be commuted to imprisonment for life.'

'Who made out the appeal for her?' I asked.

'I did,' he said. 'To be quite honest, I do not really feel she is a murderer. If you look into her face, her eyes, you

1

will never believe that so gentle a woman can commit murder.'

'Who says murder does not require that a person be gentle?'

He stared at me in surprise for a brief moment, and then laughed nervously.

'Have you ever killed anybody?'

'Am I a gentle woman?' I replied.

He turned his head to one side, pointed to a tiny window, and said, 'That's her cell. I'll go and persuade her to come down and meet you.'

After a while he came back without her. Firdaus had refused to see me.

I was supposed to examine some other women prisoners that day, but instead I got into my car and drove away.

Back home I could not do anything. I had to revise the draft of my latest book, but I was incapable of concentrating. I could think of nothing but the woman called Firdaus who, in ten days' time, would be led to the gallows.

Early next morning I found myself at the prison gates again. I asked the warder to let me see Firdaus, but she said: 'It's no use, Doctor. She will never agree to see you.'

'Why?'

'They're going to hang her in a few days' time. What use are you, or anybody else to her? Leave her alone!'

There was a note of anger in her voice. She gave me a look charged with wrath, as though I was the one who would hang Firdaus in a few days' time.

'I have nothing to do with the authorities either here or any other place,' I said.

'That's what they all say,' she said angrily.

'Why are you so worked up?' I asked. 'Do you think Firdaus is innocent, that she didn't kill him?'

She replied with an added fury, 'Murderer or not, she's an innocent woman and does not deserve to be hanged. They are the ones that ought to hang.'

'They? Who are *they*?'

She looked at me with suspicion and said, 'Tell me rather, who are you? Did they send you to her?'

'Whom do you mean by "they"?' I asked again.

She looked around cautiously, almost with fear, and stepped back away from me.

' "They" . . . You mean to say you don't know them?'

'No,' I said.

She emitted a short, sarcastic laugh and walked off. I heard her muttering to herself:

'How can she be the only one who does not know them?'

I returned to the prison several times, but all my attempts to see Firdaus were of no avail. I felt somehow that my research was now in jeopardy. As a matter of fact, my whole life seemed to be threatened with failure. My self-confidence began to be badly shaken, and I went through difficult moments. It looked to me as though this woman who had killed a human being, and was shortly to be killed herself, was a much better person than I. Compared to her, I was nothing but a small insect crawling upon the land amidst millions of other insects.

Whenever I remembered the expression in the eyes of the warder, or the prison doctor, as they spoke of her complete indifference to everything, her attitude of total rejection, and above all her refusal to see me, the feeling that I was helpless, and of no significance grew on me. A question kept turning round and round in my mind increasingly: 'What sort of woman was she? Since she had rejected me, did that mean she was a better person than me? But then, she had also refused to send an appeal to the President (Egyptian President) asking him to protect her from the gallows. Could that signify that she was better than the Head of State?'

3

I was seized by a feeling very close to certainty, yet difficult to explain, that she was, in fact, better than all the men and women we normally hear about, or see, or know.

I tried to overcome my inability to sleep, but another thought started to occupy my mind and keep me awake. When she refused to see me did she know who I was, or had she rejected me without knowing?

The following morning, I found myself back once more in the prison. I had no intention of trying to meet Firdaus, for I had given up all hope. I was looking for the warder, or the prison doctor. The doctor had not yet arrived but I found the warder.

'Did Firdaus tell you she knew me?' I asked her.

'No, she did not tell me anything,' the warder replied. 'But she does know you.'

'How do you know that she knows me?'

'I can sense her.'

I just stood there as though turned to stone. The warder left me to get on with her work. I tried to move, to go towards my car and leave, but in vain. A strange feeling of heaviness weighed down my heart, my body, drained my legs of their power. A feeling heavier than the weight of the whole earth, as though instead of standing above its surface, I was now lying somewhere beneath it. The sky also had undergone a change; its colour had turned to black, like that of the earth, and it was pressing down upon me with its added load.

It was a feeling I had known only once before, many years ago. I had fallen in love with a man who did not love me. I felt rejected, not only by him, not only by one person amongst the millions that peopled the vast world, but by every living being or thing on earth, by the vast world itself.

I straightened my shoulders, stood as upright as I could, and took a deep breath. The weight on my head lifted a little. I began to look around me and to feel amazed at finding myself in the prison at this early hour. The warder was bent double, scrubbing the tiled floor of the corridor. I was overcome by an unusual contempt towards her. She was no more than a woman cleaning the prison floor. She could not read or write and knew nothing about psychology, so how was it that I had so easily believed her feelings could be true?

Firdaus did not actually say she knew me. The warder merely sensed it. Why should that indicate that Firdaus really knew me? If she had rejected me without knowing who I was there was no reason for me to feel hurt. Her refusal to see me was not directed against me personally, but against the world and everybody in it.

I started to walk towards my car with the intention of leaving. Subjective feelings such as those that had taken hold of me were not worthy of a researcher in science. I almost smiled at myself as I opened the door of the car. The touch of its surface helped to restore my identity, my self-esteem as a doctor. Whatever the circumstances, a doctor was surely to be preferred to a woman condemned to death for murder. My normal attitude towards myself (an attitude which rarely deserts me) gradually returned. I turned the ignition key and pressed my foot down on the accelerator, firmly stamping out the sudden feeling (which occasionally haunts me in moments of failure) of merely being an insignificant insect, crawling on the earth amidst myriads of other similar insects. I heard a voice behind me, rising over the sound of the engine.

'Doctor! Doctor!'

It was the warder. She ran up to me panting heavily. Her gasping voice reminded me of the voices I often heard in my dreams. Her mouth had grown bigger, and so had her lips, which kept opening and closing with a mechanical movement, like a swing door.

I heard her say, 'Firdaus, Doctor! Firdaus wants to see you!'

Her breast was heaving up and down, her breathing had become a series of rapid gasps, and her eyes and face reflected a violent emotion. If the President of the Republic in person had asked to see me, she could not have been swept by such an overpowering emotion.

My breathing in turn quickened, as though by infection, or

to be more precise, I felt out of breath, for my heart was beating more strongly than it had ever done before. I do not know how I climbed out of the car, nor how I followed so closely behind the warder that I sometimes overtook her, or moved ahead. I walked with a rapid, effortless pace, as though my legs were no longer carrying a body. I was full of a wonderful feeling, proud, elated, happy. The sky was blue with a blueness I could capture in my eyes. I held the whole world in my hands; it was mine. It was a feeling I had known only once before, many years ago. I was on my way to meet the first man I loved for the first time.

I stopped for a moment in front of Firdaus' cell to catch my breath and adjust the collar of my dress. But I was trying to regain my composure, to return to my normal state, to the realization that I was a researcher in science, a psychiatrist, or something of the kind. I heard the key grind in the lock, brutal, screeching. The sound restored me to myself. My hand tightened its grasp on the leather bag, and a voice within me said, 'Who is this woman called Firdaus? She is only . . .'

But the words within me stopped short. Suddenly we were face to face. I stood rooted to the ground, silent, motionless. I did not hear the beat of my heart, nor the key as it turned in the lock, closing the heavy door behind me. It was as though I died the moment her eyes looked into mine. They were eyes that killed, like a knife, probing, cutting deep down inside, their look steady, unwavering. Not the slightest movement of a lid. Not the smallest twitch of a muscle in the face.

I was brought back suddenly by a voice. The voice was hers, steady, cutting deep down inside, cold as a knife. Not the slightest wavering in its tone. Not the smallest shiver of a note. I heard her say:

'Close the window.'

I moved up to the window blindly and closed it, then cast a bemused look around. There was nothing in the cell. Not a bed, or a chair, or anything on which I could sit down. I heard her say:

'Sit down on the ground.'

My body bent down and sat on the ground. It was January and the ground was bare, but I felt no cold. Like walking in one's sleep. The ground under me was cold. The same touch, the same consistency, the same naked cold. Yet the cold did not touch me, did not reach me. It was the cold of the sea in a dream. I swam through its waters. I was naked and knew not how to swim. But I neither felt its cold, nor drowned in its waters. Her voice too was like the voices one hears in a dream. It was close to me, yet seemed to come from afar, spoke from a distance and seemed to arise from nearby. For we do not know from where these voices arise: from above or below, to our left or our right. We might even think they come from the depths of the earth, drop from the rooftops, or fall from the heavens. Or they might even flow from all directions, like air moving in space reaches the ears.

But this was no dream. This was not air flowing into my ears. The woman sitting on the ground in front of me was a real woman, and the voice filling my ears with its sound, echoing in a cell where the window and door were tightly shut, could only be her voice, the voice of Firdaus.

2

Let me speak. Do not interrupt me. I have no time to listen to you. They are coming to take me at six o'clock this evening. Tomorrow morning I shall no longer be here. Nor will I be in any place known to man. This journey to a place unknown to everybody on this earth fills me with pride. All my life I have been searching for something that would fill me with pride, make me feel superior to everyone else, including kings, princes and rulers. Each time I picked up a newspaper and found the picture of a man who was one of them, I would spit on it. I knew I was only spitting on a piece of newspaper which I needed for covering the kitchen shelves. Nevertheless I spat, and then left the spit where it was to dry.

Anyone who saw me spitting on the picture might think I knew that particular man personally. But I did not. I am just one woman. And there is no single woman who could possibly know all the men who get their pictures published in the newspapers. For after all, I was only a successful prostitute. And no matter how successful a prostitute is, she cannot get to know all the men. However, all the men I did get to know, every single man of them, has filled me with but one desire: to lift my hand and bring it smashing down on his face. But because I am a woman I have never had the courage to lift my hand. And because I am a prostitute, I hid my fear under layers of make-up. Since I was successful, my make-up was always of the best and most expensive kind, just like the make-up of respectable upper-class women. I always had my hair done by stylists who tendered their services only to upper-class society women. The colour I chose for lipstick was always 'natural and serious' so that it neither disguised, nor accentuated the seductiveness of my lips. The skilful lines pencilled around my eyes hinted at just the right combination of attraction and rejection favoured by the wives of men in high positions of authority. Only my make-up, my hair and my expensive shoes were 'upper class'. With my secondary school certificate and suppressed desires I belonged to the 'middle class'. By birth I was lower class.

My father, a poor peasant farmer, who could neither read, nor write, knew very few things in life. How to grow crops, how to sell a buffalo poisoned by his enemy before it died, how to exchange his virgin daughter for a dowry when there was still time, how to be quicker than his neighbour in stealing from the fields once the crop was ripe. How to bend over the headman's hand and pretend to kiss it, how to beat his wife and make her bite the dust each night.

Every Friday morning he would put on a clean *galabeya* and head for the mosque to attend the weekly prayer. The prayer over, I would see him walking with the other men like himself as they commented on the Friday sermon, on how convincing and eloquent the *imam* had been to a degree that he had surpassed the unsurpassable. For was it not verily true that stealing was a sin, and killing was a sin, and defaming the honour of a woman was a sin, and injustice was a sin, and beating another human being was a sin . . .? Moreover, who could deny that to be obedient was a duty, and to love one's country too. That love of the ruler and love of Allah were one and indivisible. Allah protect our ruler for many long years and may he remain a source of inspiration and strength to our country, the Arab Nation and all Mankind.

I could see them walking through the narrow winding lanes, nodding their heads in admiration, and in approval of everything his Holiness the *Imam* had said. I would watch them as they continued to nod their heads, rub their hands one against the other, wipe their brows while all the time invoking Allah's name, calling upon his blessings, repeating His holy words in a guttural, subdued tone, muttering and whispering without a moment's respite.

On my head I carried a heavy earthenware jar, full of water. Under its weight my neck would sometimes jerk backwards, or to the left or to the right. I had to exert myself to maintain it balanced on my head, and keep it from falling. I kept my legs moving in the way my mother had taught me, so that my neck remained upright. I was still young at the time, and my breasts were not yet rounded. I knew nothing about men. But I could hear them as they invoked Allah's name and called upon His blessings, or repeated His holy words in a subdued guttural tone. I would observe them nodding their heads, or rubbing their hands one against the other, or coughing, or clearing their throats with a rasping noise, or constantly scratching under the armpits and between the thighs. I saw them as they watched what went on around them with wary, doubting, stealthy eyes, eyes ready to pounce, full of an aggressiveness that seemed strangely servile.

Sometimes I could not distinguish which one of them was my father. He resembled them so closely that it was difficult to tell. So one day I asked my mother about him. How was it that she had given birth to me without a father? First she beat me. Then she brought a woman who was carrying a small knife or maybe a razor blade. They cut off a piece of flesh from between my thighs.

I cried all night. Next morning my mother did not send me to the fields. She usually made me carry a load of manure on my head and take it to the fields. I preferred to go to the fields rather than stay in our hut. There, I could play with the goats, climb over the water-wheel, and swim with the boys in the stream. A little boy called Mohammadain used to pinch me under water and follow me into the small shelter made of maize stalks. He would make me lie down beneath a pile of straw, and lift up my *galabeya*. We played at 'bride and bridegroom'. From some part in my body, where, exactly I did not know, would come a sensation of sharp pleasure. Later I would close my eyes and feel with my hand for the exact spot. The moment I touched it, I would realize that I had felt the sensation before. Then we would start to play again until the sun went down, and we could hear his father's voice calling to him from the neighbouring field. I would try to hold him back, but he would run off, promising to come the next day.

But my mother no longer sent me to the fields. Before the sun had started to appear in the sky, she would nudge me in the shoulder with her fist so that I would awaken, pick up the earthenware jar and go off to fill it with water. Once back, I would sweep under the animals and then make rows of dung cakes which I left in the sun to dry. On baking day I would knead dough and make bread.

To knead the dough I squatted on the ground with the trough between my legs. At regular intervals I lifted the elastic mass up into the air and let it fall back into the trough. The heat of the oven was full on my face, singeing the edges of my hair. My *galabeya* often slipped up my thighs, but I paid no attention until the moment when I would glimpse my uncle's hand moving slowly from behind the book he was reading to touch my leg. The next moment I could feel it travelling up my thigh with a cautious, stealthy, trembling movement. Every time there was the sound of a footstep at the entrance to our house, his hand would withdraw quickly. But whenever everything around us lapsed into silence, broken only every now and then by the snap of dry twigs between my fingers as I fed the oven, and the sound of his regular breathing reaching me from behind the book so that I could not tell whether he was snoring quietly in his sleep or wide awake and panting, his hand would continue to press against my thigh with a grasping, almost brutal insistence.

He was doing to me what Mohammadain had done to me
before. In fact, he was doing even more, but I no longer felt
the strong sensation of pleasure that radiated from an
unknown and yet familiar part of my body. I closed my eyes
and tried to reach the pleasure I had known before but in
vain. It was as if I could no longer recall the exact spot
from which it used to arise, or as though a part of me, of
my being, was gone and would never return.

My uncle was not young. He was much older than I was. He
used to travel to Cairo alone, attend classes in El Azhar, and
study at a time when I was still a child and had not yet
learned to read or write. My uncle would put a chalk pencil
between my fingers and make me write on a slate: *Alif, Ba,
Gim, Dal* . . . Sometimes he made me repeat after him:
'Alif has nothing on her, Ba's got one dot underneath,
Gim's got a dot in the middle, Dal has nothing at all.' He
would nod his head as he recited from the thousand verse
poem of Ibn Malik, just as though he was reciting from the
Koran, and I would repeat each letter after him, and nod my
head in the same way.

Once the holidays were over, my uncle would climb on
the back of the donkey, and set off for the Delta Railway
Station. I followed close behind carrying his big basket,
packed full of eggs, cheese and bread cakes, topped with his
books and clothes. All along the way, until we got to the
station, my uncle would not cease talking to me about his
room at the end of Mohammad Ali Street near the Citadel,
about El Azhar, Ataba Square, the trams, the people who
lived in Cairo. At moments he would sing in a sweet voice,
his body swaying rhythmically with the movement of the
donkey.

'I abandoned ye not on the high seas
Yet on the dry land thou hast left me.
I bartered thee not for shining gold
Yet for worthless straw thou didst sell me

15

O my long night
O mine eyes. Oh.'

When my uncle would clamber into the train, and bid me farewell, I would cry and beg him to take me with him to Cairo. But my uncle would ask,

'What will you do in Cairo, Firdaus?'

And I would reply: 'I will go to El Azhar and study like you.'

Then he would laugh and explain that El Azhar was only for men. And I would cry, and hold on to his hand, as the train started to move. But he would pull it away with a force and suddenness that made me fall flat on my face.

So I would retrace my steps with bent head, pondering the shape of my toes, as I walked along the country road, wondering about myself, as the questions went round in my mind. Who was I? Who was my father? Was I going to spend my life sweeping the dung out from under the animals, carrying manure on my head, kneading dough, and baking bread?

Back in my father's house I stared at the mud walls like a stranger who had never entered it before. I looked around almost in surprise, as though I had not been born here, but had suddenly dropped from the skies, or emerged from somewhere deep down in the earth, to find myself in a place where I did not belong, in a home which was not mine, born from a father who was not my father, and from a mother who was not my mother. Was it my uncle's talk of Cairo, and the people who lived there that had changed me? Was I really the daughter of my mother, or was my mother someone else? Or was I born the daughter of my mother and later changed into someone else? Or had my mother been transformed into another woman who resembled her so closely that I could not tell the difference?

I tried to recall what my mother had looked like the first time I saw her. I can remember two eyes. I can remember her eyes in particular. I cannot describe their colour, or their shape. They were eyes that I watched. They were eyes that watched me. Even if I disappeared from their view, they

could see me, and follow me wherever I went, so that
if I faltered while learning to walk they would hold me
up.

Every time I tried to walk, I fell. A force seemed to push
me from behind, so that I fell forwards, or a weight from in
front seemed to lean on me so that I fell backwards. It was
something like a pressure of the air wanting to crush me;
something like the pull of the earth trying to suck me down
into its depths. And in the midst of it all there I was, strugg-
ling, straining my arms and legs in an attempt to stand up.
But I kept falling, buffeted by the contradictory forces that
kept pulling me in different directions, like an object thrown
into a limitless sea, without shores and without a bed, slashed
by the waters when it starts to sink, and by the wind if it
starts to float. Forever sinking and rising, sinking and rising
between the sea and the sky, with nothing to hold on to
except the two eyes. Two eyes to which I clung with all my
might. Two eyes that alone seemed to hold me up. To this
very moment I do not know whether they were wide or
narrow, nor can I recall if they were surrounded by lashes or
not. All I can remember are two rings of intense white
around two circles of intense black. I only had to look into
them for the white to become whiter and the black even
blacker, as though sunlight was pouring into them from
some magical source neither on earth, nor in the sky, for the
earth was pitch black, and the sky dark as night, with no sun
and no moon.

I could tell she was my mother, how I do not know. So
I crawled up to her seeking warmth from her body. Our hut
was cold, yet in winter my father used to shift my straw
mat and my pillow to the small room facing north, and
occupy my corner in the oven room. And instead of staying
by my side to keep me warm, my mother used to abandon
me alone and go to my father to keep him warm. In summer
I would see her sitting at his feet with a tin mug in her hand
as she washed his legs with cold water.

When I grew a little older my father put the mug in my
hand and taught me how to wash his legs with water. I had

now replaced my mother and did the things she used to do. My mother was no longer there, but instead there was another woman who hit me on my hand and took the mug away from me. My father told me she was my mother. In fact, she looked exactly like my mother; the same long garments, the same face, and the same way of moving. But when I used to look into her eyes I could feel she was not my mother. They were not the eyes that held me up each time I was on the point of falling. They were not two rings of pure white surrounding two circles of intense black, where the white would become even whiter, and the black even blacker every time I looked into them, as though the light of the sun or the moon kept flowing through them.

No light seemed ever to touch the eyes of this woman, even when the day was radiant and the sun at its very brightest. One day I took her head between my hands and turned it so that the sun fell directly on her face, but her eyes remained dull, impervious to its light, like two extinguished lamps. I stayed awake all night weeping alone, trying to muffle my sobs so that they would not disturb my little brothers and sisters sleeping on the floor beside me. For, like most people, I had many brothers and sisters. They were like chicks that multiply in spring, shiver in winter and lose their feathers, and then in summer are stricken with diarrhoea, waste away quickly and one by one creep into a corner and die.

When one of his female children died, my father would eat his supper, my mother would wash his legs, and then he would go to sleep, just as he did every night. When the child that died was a boy, he would beat my mother, then have his supper and lie down to sleep.

My father never went to bed without supper, no matter what happened. Sometimes when there was no food at home we would all go to bed with empty stomachs. But he would never fail to have a meal. My mother would hide his food from us at the bottom of one of the holes in the oven. He would sit eating alone while we watched him. One evening I dared to stretch out my hand to his plate, but he struck me a sharp blow over the back of my fingers.

I was so hungry that I could not cry. I sat in front of him watching as he ate, my eyes following his hand from the moment his fingers plunged into the bowl until it rose into the air, and carried the food into his mouth. His mouth was like that of a camel, with a big opening and wide jaws. His upper jaw kept clamping down on his lower jaw with a loud grinding noise, and chewed through each morsel so thoroughly that we could hear his teeth striking against each other. His tongue kept rolling round and round in his mouth as though it also was chewing, darting out every now and then to lick off some particle of food that had stuck to his lips, or dropped on his chin.

At the end of his meal my mother would bring him a glass of water. He drank it, then belched loudly, expelling the air from the mouth or belly with a prolonged noise. After that he smoked his water pipe, filling the room around him with thick clouds of smoke, coughing, snorting and inhaling deeply through his mouth and nose. Once over with his pipe he lay down, and a moment later the hut would resonate with his loud snoring.

I sensed he was not my father. Nobody told me, and I was not really aware of the fact. I could just feel it deep down inside me. I did not whisper the secret to anyone but kept it to myself. Every time my uncle came back for the summer holidays, I would hang on to his *gallabeya* when the time came for him to leave, and ask that he take me with him. My uncle was closer to me than my father. He was not so old, and he allowed me to sit beside him and look at his books. He taught me the alphabet, and after my father died he sent me to elementary school. Later, when my mother died, he took me with him to Cairo.

I sometimes wonder whether a person can be born twice. When I entered my uncle's dwelling, I put my hand on a switch and light flooded the room. I shut my eyes against the glare and screamed. When I opened my lids again I had the feeling of looking out through them for the first time, as though I had just come into the world, or was being born a second time, since I knew that I had in fact been born some years before. I glimpsed myself in the mirror. This also had never happened to me before. At first I did not know that it was a mirror. I was frightened when I found myself looking at a little girl wearing a dress that reached down no further than her knees, and a pair of shoes that hid her feet. I looked round the room. There was no one else in it apart from me. I could not understand where this girl had sprung from, nor realize that she could only be me. For I was always dressed in a long *gallabeya* which trailed along the ground, and no matter where I went it was always barefoot. But I recognized my face immediately. Yet how could I be so sure it was my face since I had not seen myself in a mirror before? The room was empty, and the wardrobe mirror was right in front of me. This girl standing upright in it could only be me. The dress and the shoes had been bought by my uncle for me to wear in school.

I stood in front of the mirror staring at my face. Who am I? Firdaus, that is how they call me. The big round nose I got from my father, and the thin-lipped mouth from my mother.

A sinking feeling went through my body. I neither liked the look of my nose, nor the shape of my mouth. I thought my father had died, yet here he was alive in the big, ugly, rounded nose. My mother, too, was dead, but continued to live in the form of this thin-lipped mouth. And here I was unchanged, the same Firdaus, but now clad in a dress, and with shoes on her feet.

I was filled with a deep hatred for the mirror. From that moment I never looked into it again. Even when I stood in front of it, I was not seeing myself but only combing my hair, or wiping my face, or adjusting the collar of my dress. Then I would pick up my satchel and race off to school.

I loved school. It was full of boys and girls. We played in the courtyard, gasping for breath as we ran from one end of it to the other, or sat splitting sunflower seeds between our teeth in rapid succession, or chewed gum with a loud smacking noise, or bought molass sugar sticks and dry *carob*, or drank liquorice and tamarind and sugar cane juice; in other words, we went for everything with a deliciously strong flavour.

Once back I would sweep and clean the house, wash my uncle's clothes, make his bed, and tidy his books. He bought me a heavy iron which I would heat on the kerosene stove, and use to launder his kaftan and turban. Shortly before sunset he would return from El Azhar. I served supper and we ate it together. The meal over, I lay on my sofa, while my uncle sat on his bed and read out aloud. I used to jump up to his side on the high bed, curl my fingers around his large hand with its long, thin fingers and touch his great big books, with their smooth, closely written pages, covered in fine black letters. I would try to make out a few words. They looked to me like mysterious signs that filled me with something like fear. El Azhar was an awesome world peopled only by men, and my uncle was one of them, was a man. When he read, his voice resonated with a sacred awe, and his great long fingers were seized with a strange trembling which I could feel under my hand. It was familiar, like a trembling experienced in childhood, a distant dream still remembered.

During the cold winter nights, I curled up in my uncle's arms like a baby in its womb. We drew warmth from our closeness. My face buried in his arms, I wanted to tell him that I loved him, but the words would not come. I wanted to cry but the tears would not flow. And after a while I would fall into a deep sleep until morning.

One day I fell sick with fever. My uncle sat on the bed by my side holding my head, patting my face gently with his great long fingers, and I slept all night holding on to his hand.

When I was awarded my primary school certificate he bought me a little wrist watch, and that night took me to the cinema. I saw a woman dancing. Her thighs were naked. And I saw a man hugging a woman. Then he kissed her on the lips. I hid my face behind my hand and did not dare to look at my uncle. Later, he told me that dancing was a sin, and that kissing a man, too, was a sin, but now I could no longer look into his eyes. That night when we returned home I did not sit beside him on the bed as I often used to do before, but hid myself under the eiderdown on my little sofa.

I was trembling all over, seized with a feeling I could not explain, that my uncle's great long fingers would draw close to me after a little while, and cautiously lift the eiderdown under which I lay. Then his lips would touch my face and press down on my mouth, and his trembling fingers would feel their way slowly upwards over my thighs.

A strange thing was happening to me, strange because it had never happened to me before, or because it had been happening to me all the time, ever since I could remember. Somewhere, in some distant spot within my body was awakening an old pleasure lost a long time ago, or a new pleasure still unknown, and indefinable, for it seemed to arise outside my body, or in a part of my being severed from it many years ago.

My uncle started to go out a lot. When I woke up in the morning he would be gone, and when he came back at night

22

I would be in bed, fast asleep. If I brought him a glass of water, or a plate of food, he would stretch out his hand, and take it, without looking at me. When I hid my head under the eiderdown, I would listen intently for the sound of his footsteps. I held my breath and pretended to be asleep, waiting for his fingers to reach out for me. An eternity seemed to pass without anything happening. I could hear his bed creak as he lay down, followed after some time by the sound of his regular snoring. Then, only, was I assured that he had fallen asleep.

He became a different man. He no longer read before going to sleep, or wore his *jebbah* and kaftan. Instead he bought a suit and tie, found a post in the Ministry of Wakfs, and married the daughter of his teacher at El Azhar.

He sent me to secondary school, and took me with him to his new house, where I lived with him and his wife. His wife was a short, fat woman with a fair complexion. Her sluggish body swayed from side to side when she walked, with the waddling movement of a well-fed duck. Her voice was soft not with gentleness, but with the softness born of cruelty. Her eyes were large, and black with an extinguished vitality that left nothing but pools of dark, sleepy indifference.

She never washed my uncle's feet, and he never beat her, or spoke to her in a loud voice. He was extremely polite, but treated her with the peculiar kind of courtesy devoid of true respect which men preserve for women. I sensed that his feeling for her was more one of fear than of love, and that she came from a higher social class than his. When her father, or one of her relatives paid us a visit my uncle would buy meat or chicken, and the house would resonate with his laughter. But when his aunt arrived, dressed in her flowing peasant garments, her cracked hands showing through the openings of her long sleeves, he retreated into a corner without a word or even a smile.

His aunt would sit next to me on the bed weeping silently, and mentioning how she regretted having sold her golden necklace in order to pay for his studies in El Azhar. In the morning she would empty her basket of the chicken, eggs and breadcakes it contained, hook it over her arm, and leave. I would say to her,

'Stay just another day with us, Grandma,' but my uncle never said a word, and neither did his wife.

I went to school every day. Once back I swept the house and washed the floor, the dishes and the clothes. My uncle's wife only did the cooking, leaving the pots and pans for me to scour and clean. Later, my uncle brought home a small servant girl who slept in my room. The bed was reserved for me, so she slept on the floor. On a cold night I told her to come and sleep with me in the bed, but when my uncle's wife entered the room and saw us, she beat her. Then she beat me also.

One day when I returned from school, I found my uncle looking very angry with me. His wife also seemed to share his anger, and she continued to appear angry, until he decided to take me away from the house with my clothes and books, and put me in the boarding girls section of the school. From then on I slept there at night. At the end of each week, the fathers, mothers and other relatives of the girls visited them, or took them off to spend Thursday and Friday at home. I would look over the top of the high wall and watch them as they departed, my eyes following the people and the movement of the street like a prisoner condemned to look out at life over the top of a high prison wall.

But I came to love school despite everything. There were new books, and new subjects, and girls of my age with whom I used to study. We talked to one another about our lives, exchanged secrets, and revealed our depths to one another. There was nobody to upset things for us except the superintendent who walked around the boarding house on tiptoe, spying on us day and night, listening to what we had to say. Even when we slept she kept a vigilant eye on our every movement, followed us as we dreamed. If one of us so much as sighed, or emitted a sound, or made the slightest movement in her dream, she would pounce on her like a bird of prey.

I had a friend called Wafeya. Her bed was next to mine. I would move my bed close up to hers after the lights went out, and we would talk until midnight. She spoke of a cousin with whom she was in love, and who in turn loved her, and I spoke of my hopes for the future. There was nothing in my past, or in my childhood, to talk about, and no love or anything of the sort in the present. If I had something to say, therefore, it could only concern the future. For the future was still mine to paint in the colours I desired. Still mine to decide about freely, and change as I saw fit.

Sometimes I imagined that I would become a doctor, or an engineer, or a lawyer, or a judge. And one day the whole school went out on the streets to join a big demonstration against the government. Suddenly I found myself riding high up on the shoulders of the girls shouting,

'Down with the government.'

When I got back to school my voice was hoarse, my hair in disarray, and my clothes were torn in several places, but all through the night I kept imagining myself as a great leader or head of state.

I knew that women did not become heads of state, but I felt that I was not like other women, nor like the other girls around me who kept talking about love, or about men. For these were subjects I never mentioned. Somehow I was not interested in the things that occupied their minds, and what seemed of importance to them struck me as being trivial.

One night, Wafeya asked me: 'Have you ever fallen in love, Firdaus?'

'No, Wafeya. I have never been in love,' I replied.

She stared at me with surprise and said, 'How strange!'

'Why do you find it strange?' I asked.

'There is something about your looks that suggests you are

in love.'

'But what is it in a person's looks that can hint at love?'

She shook her head and said, 'I do not know. But I feel that you, in particular, are a person who cannot live without love.'

'Yet I am living without love.'

'Then you are either living a lie, or not living at all.'

She pronounced the last word and then immediately dropped fast asleep. My eyes remained wide open, staring into the darkness. Slowly, distant, half-forgotten images started to emerge from the night. I saw Mohammadain lying on a bed of straw under the open shelter. The smell of the straw crept up my nose, and the touch of his fingers moved over my body. My whole body shuddered with a far away yet familiar pleasure arising from some unknown source, from some indefinable spot outside my being. And yet I could feel it somewhere in my body, a gentle pulsation beginning like a tender pleasure, and ending like a tender pain. Something I tried to hold on to, to touch if only for a moment, but it slipped away from me like the air, like an illusion, or a dream that floats away and is lost. I wept in my sleep as though it was something I was losing now; a loss I was experiencing for the first time, and not something I had lost a long time ago.

The nights at school were long, and the days were even longer. I would finish studying my lessons hours before the last night-bell was rung. So I discovered that the school had a library. A neglected room in the back yard, with its shelves falling to pieces, and books covered in a thick layer of dust. I used to wipe off the dust with a yellow cloth, sit on a broken chair under the light of a feeble lamp, and read.

I developed a love of books, for with every book I learned something new. I got to know about the Persians, the Turks and the Arabs. I read about the crimes committed by kings and rulers, about wars, peoples, revolutions, and the lives of revolutionaries. I read love stories and love poems. But I preferred books written about rulers. I read about a ruler whose female servants and concubines were as numerous as his army, and about another whose only interests in life were wine, women, and whipping his slaves. A third cared little for women, but enjoyed wars, killing, and torturing men. Another of these rulers loved food, money and hoarding riches without end. Still another was possessed with such an admiration for himself and his greatness that for him no one else in the land existed. There was also a ruler so obsessed with plots and conspiracies that he spent all his time distorting the facts of history and trying to fool his people.

I discovered that all these rulers were men. What they had in common was an avaricious and distorted personality, a never-ending appetite for money, sex and unlimited power. They were men who sowed corruption on the earth, and plundered their peoples, men endowed with loud voices, a capacity for persuasion, for choosing sweet words and shooting poisoned arrows. Thus, the truth about them was revealed only after their death, and as a result I discovered that history tended to repeat itself with a foolish obstinacy.

Newspapers and magazines were delivered to the library regularly. I got into the habit of reading what was written in them and looking at the pictures. And so, quite often, I would stumble on the picture of one or other of these rulers as he sat with the congregation attending Friday morning prayers. There he sat opening and closing his lids, looking out through them with an expression of great humility, like a man stricken to his depths. I could see he was trying to deceive Allah in the same way as he deceived the people. Around him were gathered members of his retinue, nodding their heads in agreement and with admiration for everything that was being said, invoking Allah's blessings and his eternal majesty in subdued guttural tones, rubbing their hands one against the other, observing what went on around them with wary, doubting, stealthy eyes, ready to pounce, full of an aggressiveness that touched on the servile.

I could see them as they prayed ardently for the souls of the nation's martyrs who had lost their lives as a result of war, famine or pestilence. I would follow the heads going down, and the buttocks coming up, fat rounded buttocks swollen with flesh and fear. When they pronounced the word 'patriotism' I could tell at once that in their heart of hearts they feared not Allah, and that at the back of their minds patriotism meant that the poor should die to defend the land of the rich, their land, for I knew that the poor had no land.

When I became bored with reading history, which seemed unchanging, bored with the same old stories, the same pictures which all looked the same, I would go down to sit in the playground all alone. Often, the night would be dark, without a moon shedding its light from above, the last bell would have pealed out its last note a long while ago, leaving a deep silence behind. Around me, all the windows would be shut, and all the lights would be out, yet I would continue to sit in the dark alone, and wonder about many things. What will become of me in the coming years? Will I go to the university? Would my uncle agree to send me there for my studies?

One night a teacher saw me as I sat there. For a moment she was frightened by the sight of a mass that did not move, yet looked like a human shape sitting in the dark. Before coming nearer to me she called out:

'Who is sitting there?'

In a weak, scared voice I replied, 'It's me, Firdaus.'

When she had drawn nearer she recognized me, and seemed surprised, for I was one of the best girls in her class, and the best girls used to go to bed as soon as the night-bell rang.

I told her I was feeling a little tense and had not been able to fall asleep, so she sat down next to me. Her name was Iqbal. She was short, and plump with long black hair and black eyes. I could see her eyes looking at me, observing me, despite the darkness. Every time I turned my head, they were after me, holding on to me, refusing to let me go. Even when I covered my face with both hands, they seemed to see through them into my eyes.

Without warning, I burst into tears. The tears ran down my face behind my hands. She took hold of both my hands and lifted them away from my face. I heard her say:

'Firdaus, Firdaus, please do not cry.'

'Let me cry,' I said.

'I've never seen you cry before. What's happened to you?'

'Nothing, nothing at all.'

'Impossible. Something must have happened.'

'No, nothing has happened Miss Iqbal.'

There was a note of surprise in her voice. 'Are you crying for no reason at all?'

'I do not know what the reason is. Nothing new has happened to me.'

She remained by my side, seated in silence. I could see her black eyes wandering into the night, and the tears welling up in them with a glistening light. She tightened her lips and swallowed hard and suddenly the light in her eyes went out. Again and again they started to shine and after a moment went out, like flames snuffed out in the night. But the moment came when she tightened her lips and swallowed hard, but in vain, for two tears stayed behind in her eyes. I saw them drop on to her nose and slowly trickle down each side. She hid her face with one hand, pulled out a handkerchief with the other and dabbed her nose.

'Are you crying, Miss Iqbal?' I asked.

'No,' she said, then hid her handkerchief, swallowed hard, and smiled at me.

The night around us was deep, silent, motionless, with not a single sound or movement anywhere. Everything was steeped in an absolute darkness through which no ray of light penetrated, for in the sky was neither moon nor sun. My face was turned towards her, and my eyes looked into her eyes: two rings of pure white, surrounding two circles of intense black, that looked out at me. As I continued to gaze into them, the white seemed to turn even whiter, and the black even blacker, as though light flowed through them from some unknown magical source which was neither on the earth, nor in the heavens, for the earth was enveloped in the cloak of night, and the heavens had no sun nor moon to give them light.

I held her eyes in mind, took her hand in mine. The feeling of our hands touching was strange, sudden. It was a feeling that made my body tremble with a deep distant pleasure, more distant than the age of my remembered life, deeper than the consciousness I had carried with me throughout. I could feel it somewhere, like a part of my being which had been born with me when I was born, but had not grown with me when I had grown, like a part of my being that I had once known, but left behind when I was born. A cloudy awareness of something that could have been, and yet was never lived.

At that moment a memory came to my mind. My lips opened to speak, but my voice failed to come through, as though no sooner did I remember than I had already forgotten. My heart faltered, stifled by a frightened, frenzied beating over something precious I was on the point of losing, or had just lost, for ever. My fingers held on to her hand with such violence that no force on earth, no matter how great, could tear it away from me.

After that night, whenever we met, my lips parted to say something which no sooner remembered was already forgotten. My heart beat with fear, or with an emotion resembling fear. I wanted to reach out to her, and take her hand, but she would enter the classroom and leave it after the lesson was over without seeming to have noticed my presence. When she happened to look at me, it was always in the same way as she looked at any other of her pupils.

In bed, before going to sleep, I used to wonder: 'Has Miss Iqbal forgotten?' A moment later Wafeya would draw her bed close to mine and ask:

'Forgotten what?'

'I don't know, Wafeya.'

'You are living in a world of imagination, Firdaus.'

'Not at all, Wafeya. It did happen, you know.'

'What happened?' she enquired.

I tried to explain to her what had happened, but I did not know how to describe it, or to be more precise I found nothing to talk about. It was as if something had happened which I was unable to recall, or as if nothing had happened at all.

I closed my eyes and tried to bring back the scene. Slowly there appeared two circles of intense black surrounded by two rings of pure white. The more I stared into them the bigger they grew, expanding before my eyes. The black circle kept growing until it reached the size of the earth, and the white circle expanded into a piercingly white mass, large as the sun. My eyes lost themselves in the black and the white until, blinded by their intensity, they could no longer perceive either one or the other. The images before my eyes became confused. I could no longer distinguish between the faces of my father and my mother, my uncle and Mohammadain, Iqbal and Wafeya. I opened my eyes wide in panic as if threatened with blindness. I could see the out-lines of Wafeya's face in front of me in the darkness. She was still awake, and I heard her say:

'Firdaus, are you in love with Miss Iqbal?'

'Me?' I said with amazement.

'Yes, you. Who else then?'

'Never, Wafeya.'

'Then why do you talk about her every night?'

'Me? Talk about her? That's not true. You always exaggerate, Wafeya.'

'Miss Iqbal is an excellent teacher,' she commented.

'Yes,' I agreed, 'but she's a woman. How could I be in love with a woman?'

There were only a few days left to the final examination. Wafeya no longer talked to me about her sweetheart, and the night-bell no longer rang as early as before. Every night I would sit up late in the study room with Wafeya and the other girls. Now and then the superintendent of the boarding house would walk in to inspect the way we studied, just as she used to walk around and inspect the way we slept or even dreamt. For if one of the girls so much as lifted her head to take a breath, or rest her neck, she would appear suddenly out of nowhere, and the girl would immediately bend her head over the book again.

I liked classes, and I enjoyed studying, despite the unfailing vigilance of the superintendent, and other things. When the results of the final examination were announced, I was told that I had come out second in the school and seventh countrywide. On the night when the certificates were distributed, a special ceremony was held for the occasion. The Principal called out my name in the big hall crowded with hundreds of mothers, fathers, and other relatives of the girls, but no one stepped up to take the certificate. A sudden silence descended on the hall. The Principal called out my name a second time. I tried to stand up but my legs failed me. I called out from my seat,

'Present.'

I saw all heads turn towards me, and all eyes staring in my direction, countless eyes transformed under my gaze into innumerable rings of white surrounding innumerable circles of black, which turned in a concerted circular movement to fix their look steadily in my eyes.

The Principal called out in a commanding voice:

'Don't reply while seated. Stand up!'

I realized that I was on my feet when the white rings and the black circles moved upwards in unison to fasten themselves once more on my eyes.

The Principal called out again in a loud voice that echoed in my ears louder than any voice I had ever heard in my life before, 'Where is your guardian?'

A heavy silence descended on the hall, a silence which seemed to possess a resonance of its own. The air vibrated with a peculiar sound, and the breathing of many chests had a rhythmic tone which reached me at the back of the crowded hall. The heads swung back to their normal position, and there I stood contemplating line upon line of backs sitting upright in their rows.

Two eyes — two eyes alone fastened themselves upon mine. No matter how far I shifted my gaze, or how much I moved my head, they followed me closely, tightened their hold. Everything was now enveloped in a growing darkness in which I could no longer discern the slightest glimmer of light, except for two jet black eyes encircled by two rings of dazzling white. The more I gazed into them the more intense the black and the white became, as though imbued with light from some magic source, for the hall was enveloped in total darkness, and the night outside was like liquid coal.

It seemed to me as though I reached out in the dark and took her hand, or that she reached out in the dark and took my hand. The sudden contact made my body shiver with a pain so deep that it was almost like pleasure, or a pleasure so deep that it bordered on pain. It was a remote pleasure, buried in such far away depths that it seemed to have arisen a very long time ago, longer than the length of memory, older than the remembered years of life's journey. Something no sooner remembered than forgotten, as if it had happened just once before, only to be lost for all time, or as though it had never happened at all.

I parted my lips ready to tell her all, but she said,

'Don't say anything Firdaus.'

She led me by the hand, through row upon row of people, until we mounted the platform where the Principal was standing. She took my certificate, then signed her name to acknowledge that she had also been given my certificate of merit. The Principal read out the marks I had received in each subject, and I heard a clatter in the hall that resembled applause. The Principal held out her hand with a box wrapped in coloured paper and tied with a silken green ribbon. I tried to stretch out my arm but it failed to move. Once more I glimpsed Miss Iqbal approaching the Principal. She took the package from her hand, then led me back through the rows of people to where I was sitting before. I sat down, put the certificate on my lap, and placed the box on top of it.

The school year had come to an end. Fathers and guardians arrived to take the girls home. The Principal sent a telegram to my uncle and a few days later he arrived at the school to take me away. I had not seen Miss Iqbal since the night of the ceremony. That same night when the 'lights out' bell rang

I was unable to sleep I slipped down to the courtyard and sat there in the dark by myself. Each time I heard a sound coming from some distance away, or felt some movement, I looked around me. At one moment I saw a shape about the size of a person moving near the entrance. I leapt to my feet. My heart beat wildly and the blood rushed to my head. It seemed to me that the shape I had seen was moving towards me. I rose and walked to meet it slowly. As I advanced I realized that my whole body was bathed in sweat, including the roots of my hair and the palms of my hands. I was alone in the darkness and a slight shiver of fear went through me. I called out, 'Miss Iqbal,' but all I managed was a mere whisper that failed even to reach my ears. I could hear nothing and my fear increased. But still there was a shape the size of a human body, looming in the dark. I spoke out in a loud voice which reached my ears clearly this time.

'Who is there?'

My own voice awakened me from what appeared to be a dream, like a person talking out loud in his sleep. The darkness seemed to lift slightly revealing a low unplastered brick wall about the height of an average person. It was a wall which I had seen before, yet for a brief moment I felt as though it had been built that instant.

Before leaving school for the last time, I kept looking around me, sweeping walls, windows, doors with my eyes unceasingly, expecting something to open suddenly and reveal her eyes, as they looked out at me for a moment, or her hand waving a usual farewell. I searched on frantically, without respite. At every moment I kept losing hope, only to regain it an instant later. My eyes shifted restlessly up and down, to and fro. My chest was heaving with a deep emotion. Before we passed through the outer gate I gasped to my uncle:

'Please wait for me just one more minute.'

The next instant I was following him into the street, and the door had already closed behind us. But I continued to turn round and look back at it for quite a while as if it was about to swing open again, or as though I had a feeling of certainty that someone was standing behind it and getting ready to push it open at any moment.

I walked with heavy steps behind my uncle, carrying the image of that closed door engraved in my mind. When I ate my meals, or drank, or lay down to sleep it was there in front of me. I knew that I was now back in my uncle's house. The woman who lived with him was his wife, and the children who ran around the house were their children. There was no place for me in this house except on the sofa, a small wooden couch placed in the dining room close up against the thin wall which separated it from the bedroom. And so every night I could hear their subdued voices whispering on the other side of the partition.

'It's not easy to find work these days when all you have is a secondary school certificate.'

'What can she do then?'

'Nothing. These secondary schools don't teach them anything. I should have sent her to a commercial training school.'

'It's no use talking of what you should have done. What are you going to do now?'

'She can stay with us until I find her a job.'

'That could be for years. The house is small and life is expensive. She eats twice as much as any of our children.'

'She helps you with the house and the children.'

'We have the servant girl, and I cook. We don't need her.'

'But she can make the work easier for you by helping with the cooking.'

'I don't like her cooking. You know, your holiness, cooking is the "spirit you breathe" into it. And I do not like what she "breathes" into her cooking, and neither do you. Don't you remember the okra she cooked for us? You told me it was not the okra you are accustomed to eat when I make it

35

with my own hands.'

'If you keep her instead of Saadia, we'll save the girl's wages.'

'She will not be able to replace Saadia. Saadia is light and quick, and puts her heart into her work. In addition, she's not too fond of food, or of sleeping long hours. But this girl's every movement is slow and heavy. She's cold-blooded and couldn't care less.'

'So what do we do with her then?'

'We can be rid of her by sending her to the university. There she can live in the quarters allocated to the girl students.'

'To the university? To a place where she will be sitting side by side with men? A respected Sheikh and man of religion like myself sending his niece off to mix in the company of men?! Besides, where will the money come from for her lodging, and books, and clothes? You know how high the cost of living is these days. Prices seem to have gone mad, and yet the salary of us government officials only rises by a few millimes.'

'Your holiness, I have a wonderful idea.'

'What is it?'

'My uncle, Sheikh Mahmoud, is a virtuous man. He has a big pension and no children, and he's been on his own since his wife died last year. If he marries Firdaus she will have a good life with him, and he can find in her an obedient wife, who will serve him and relieve his loneliness. Firdaus has grown, your holiness, and must be married. It is risky for her to continue without a husband. She is a good girl but the world is full of bastards.'

'I agree with you, but Sheikh Mahmoud is much too old for her.'

'Who said he is old! He only went on pension this year, and Firdaus herself is not that young. Girls of her age have already married years ago and borne children. An old but reliable man is surely better than a young man who treats her in a humiliating way, or beats her. You know how young men are these days.'

'I agree with you. But you must not forget the very obvious deformity he has on his face.'

'Deformity? Who says it's a deformity? Besides, your holiness, as the saying goes, "nothing shames a man but an empty pocket".'

'Supposing Firdaus refuses him?'

'Why should she refuse him? This is her best chance to get married. Do not forget what a nose she has. It's big and ugly like a tin mug. Besides, she has inherited nothing, and has no income of her own. We will never find a better husband for her than Sheikh Mahmoud.'

'Do you think Sheikh Mahmoud will welcome the idea?'

'If I speak to him I am sure he will agree. I intend to ask him for a big dowry.'

'How much?'

'A hundred pounds, or perhaps even two hundred if he has the money.'

'If he pays a hundred pounds, then Allah will indeed have been generous to us, and I would not be so greedy as to ask for more.'

'I'll start with two hundred. You know he's a man who can argue for hours over five millimes, and kill himself over a piastre.'

'If he accepts to pay one hundred pounds that will be sufficient blessing from Allah. I will be able to pay my debts and buy some underwear, as well as a dress or two for Firdaus. We cannot let her get married in the clothes she's wearing.'

'Anyhow, you won't have to worry about the bride's outfit, or furniture and utensils. Sheikh Mahmoud's house has everything in it and the furniture his late wife left behind is good, solid stuff, much better than the rubbish you get nowadays.'

'To be sure. What you say is the very truth.'

'I can swear by Allah, your holiness, that the Lord must really love this niece of yours, for she will be really fortunate if Sheikh Mahmoud agrees to marry her.'

'Do you think he will?'

'And why should he refuse indeed? Through this marriage he will become related to a respected Sheikh and man of religion. Is that not in itself reason enough for him to welcome such a proposal?'

'Maybe he's thinking of taking a woman from a wealthy family. You know how he worships the piastre.'

'And does your holiness consider himself a poor man. We are better off than a lot of people. Thanks be to Allah for everything.'

'Verily, we are full of gratitude to Allah for everything he has bestowed on us. May He be forever praised and exalted. Verily our hearts are indeed full of thanks to Allah the Almighty.'

As I lay there on the couch I heard him kiss his hand twice in rapid succession as he repeated,

'Verily our hearts are indeed full of thanks to Allah the Almighty.'

In my imagination I could almost see him kiss the palm of his hand, then turn it over to imprint a second kiss on the back. Through the thin wall, the sucking sound of the two kisses reached me one after the other, and a moment later resumed as he moved his lips over to his wife's hand, or perhaps her arm or her leg, for I now began to hear her protesting:

'No, your holiness, no,' as she pulled her arm or leg away from his embrace.

His voice followed, muttering in a subdued, soft tone almost like a short run of new kisses,

'No what, you woman?'

The bed creaked under them, and now I could hear their breathing, irregular, panting, and her voice as she protested once again:

'No, your holiness, for the sake of the Prophet. No,this is sinful.'

Then his stifled tones hissing back:

'You woman, you . . . What sin, and what Prophet? I'm your husband and you're my wife.'

The bed creaked even more loudly under the two heavy

bodies locked in a struggle, alternately closing in on one another and separating in a continuous movement, slow and heavy at first, then gradually shifting to a strangely rapid, almost frenzied rhythm that shook the bed, and the floor, and the wall between us and even the sofa on which I was lying. I felt my body vibrate with the sofa, my breathing grew more rapid, so that after a while I also started to pant with the same strange frenzy. Then slowly, as their movements subsided their respiration grew quiet again, and I gradually became calmer. My breathing resumed its normal slow regularity, and I dropped off to sleep with my body bathed in a pool of sweat.

The following morning I made breakfast for my uncle. He raised his eyes to look at me whenever I brought him a glass, or a cup of water, but each time I would turn my face in another direction to avoid his eyes. I waited until he left, then I kneeled under the wooden couch, pulled out my shoes, slipped my feet into them and put on my dress. I opened my small bag, folded my nightgown, packed it inside, and placed my secondary school certificate and my certificate of merit on top before closing it. My uncle's wife was in the kitchen cooking, and Saadia the servant girl was feeding the children in their room. Hala, the youngest of my cousins, came in at that moment. Her black eyes opened wide, staring at my dress, shoes and little bag. She had not learned to talk yet and could not pronounce the name Firdaus, so she used to call me 'Daus'. She was the only one of the children who smiled at me, and when I was alone in the room, she would come in and jump on to the couch and say,

'Daus, Daus.'

I would stroke her hair and answer, 'Yes, Hala.'

'Daus, Daus,' she would reply, and giggle, and then try to make me play with her. But her mother's voice would soon be heard calling to her from outside, so she would jump off the couch, and toddle away on her little legs.

Hala's eyes were shifting continuously from my shoes, to my dress, to my little bag and then back. She was holding on to the hem of my dress, and kept saying:

'Daus, Daus.'

I whispered in her ear, 'I'm coming back, Hala.'

But she would not keep quiet. Her fingers held to my hand and she continued to repeat, 'Daus, Daus.'

I gave her a picture of myself to keep her occupied, opened the door of the flat, stepped out, and closed it silently behind me. I heard her voice calling out from behind the door:

'Daus, Daus.'

My feet ran down the stairs, but her voice continued to echo in my ears until I reached the bottom, and walked out into the street. As I advanced over the pavement I could still hear it coming from somewhere behind me. I turned round, but could see no one.

I walked down the street just as I had done many times before, but this time it felt different for I did not have any particular destination. In fact, I had no idea where my steps were leading me. When I looked at the streets it was as though I was seeing them for the first time. A new world was opening up in front of my eyes, a world which for me had not existed before. Maybe it had always been there, always existed, but I had never seen it, never realized it had been there all the time. How was it that I had been blind to its existence all these years? Now it seemed as if a third eye had suddenly been slit open in my head. I could see crowds of people moving in an incessant flow through the streets, some walking on their legs, others riding in buses and cars. All of them were in a hurry, rushing along, oblivious of what was happening around them. No one noticed me as I stood there alone. And because they did not notice me I was able to observe them well. There were people walking on the street who wore shabby, torn clothes and downtrodden shoes. Their faces were pale, their eyes dull, resigned, weighed down with a certain sadness and worry. But those who rode in cars had broad, fleshy shoulders, and their cheeks were full and rounded. From behind the glass windows they looked out with wary, doubting, stealthy eyes, eyes preparing to pounce and full of aggression yet bordering on the strangely servile. I could not distinguish the faces, or the eyes of those who rode in the buses, only their heads, and their backs which I could see crowded against each other, filling up the whole space of the bus, overflowing on to the steps and the roof. When the bus came to a stop at the station, or slowed down I could glimpse the jaundiced faces shining with sweat, and the bulging eyes expressing a certain fear.

I was amazed by the huge number of people filling up the streets everywhere, but even more amazed to see the way they moved around like blind creatures that could neither see themselves, nor anyone else. My amazement became even greater when I suddenly realized that I had become one of them. This realization filled me with a sensation that at first had something most pleasurable about it, but quickly changed like the wonderment of an infant that opens its eyes for the first time to perceive the world around, and yet the very next moment bursts out screaming as it feels itself projected into a new environment where it had never been before.

When night fell I had not yet found a place where I could spend the long hours until morning. I felt something deep inside of me screaming with panic. I was now worn out with fatigue, my stomach racked with hunger. I rested my back against a wall and stood for a while looking around me. I could see the wide expanse of street stretched out before me like the sea. There I was, just a pebble which someone had tossed into its waters, rolling along with the crowds that rode in buses and cars, or walked the streets, with unseeing eyes, incapable of noticing anything or anyone. Each minute a thousand eyes passed in front of me, but for them I remained non-existent.

In the dark I suddenly perceived two eyes, or rather felt them, moving towards me very slowly, closer and closer. They dropped their gaze with slow intent down to my shoes, rested there for a moment, then gradually started to climb up my legs, to my thighs, my belly, my breasts, my neck and finally came to a stop, fastening themselves steadily in my eyes, with the same cold intent.

A shudder passed through my body, like the fear of death, or like death itself. I tensed the muscles in my back and face to stay the shiver and overcome this feeling of terror which had swept my whole being. For after all, I was not confronted with a hand holding a knife or a razor, but only with two eyes, nothing but two eyes. I swallowed with an effort, and thrust one leg forward. I was able to move my body a few steps away from the eyes, but I felt them on my back, boring through me from behind. I noticed a small shop lit up by a glaring light, and hastened my pace towards it. I stepped inside and hid amidst the little crowd. A few moments later I came out and looked up and down the street cautiously. When I was sure the eyes had gone, I ran quickly down the pavement. Now I had but one thought in my mind. How to reach my uncle's house in the shortest possible time.

Once back I do not know how I put up with life in my uncle's house, nor do I remember how I became Sheikh Mahmoud's wife. All I know is that anything I would have to face in the world had become less frightening than the vision of those two eyes, which sent a cold shiver running through my spine whenever I remembered them. I had no idea what colour they were, green or black, or something else. Nor could I recall their shape, whether they were large, wide-open eyes, or just two narrow slits. But whenever I walked in the street, whether by day or by night, I would look around me carefully as though I expected the two eyes to rise up suddenly through some opening in the ground and confront me.

The day came when I departed from my uncle's house and went to live with Sheikh Mahmoud. Now I slept on a comfortable bed instead of the wooden couch. But no sooner did I stretch out my body on it to rest from the fatigue of cooking, and washing and cleaning the large house with its rooms full of furniture, than Sheikh Mahmoud would appear by my side. He was already over sixty, whereas I had not yet turned nineteen. On his chin, below the lip, was a large swelling, with a hole in the middle. Some days the hole would be dry, but on others it would turn into a rusty old tap exuding drops red in colour like blood, or whitish yellow, like pus.

When the hole dried up, I let him kiss me. I could feel the swelling on my face and lips like a small purse, or a water skin, full of a stagnant greasy fluid. But on days when it was not dry I would turn my lips and face away to avoid the odour of dead dogs which emanated from it.

At night he would wind his legs and arms around me, and let his old, gnarled hand travel all over my body, like the claws of a starving man who has been deprived of real food for many years wipe the bowl of food clean, and leave not a single crumb behind.

He lacked the ability to eat much. The swelling on his face interfered with the movement of his jaws, and his shrivelled old man's stomach was upset by too much food. Although he could only eat small amounts, yet each time he would wipe his plate clean, sweeping the piece of bread held between his fingers round and round to make sure nothing was left. He kept looking at my plate while I ate, and if I left anything over he picked it up, put it in his mouth and after swallowing, quickly told me off for my wastefulness. Yet I was not given to wasting anything, and the only food I left on the plate were the scanty remains which stuck to its surface, and could only be removed with soap and water.

When his arms and legs let go of me, I would gently slip my body out from under him, and go on tiptoe to the bathroom. There I would carefully wash my face and lips, my arms and thighs, and every part of my body, taking care not to miss a single inch, going over it several times with soap and water.

He had retired from his job, was without work, and without friends. He never went out of the house, or sat at a coffee-house, lest he be obliged to pay a few piastres for a cup of coffee. All day long he remained by my side in the house, or in the kitchen, watching me as I cooked or washed. If I dropped the packet of soap powder and spilled a few grains on the floor, he would jump up from his chair and complain at me for being careless. And if I pressed a little more firmly than usual on the spoon as I took ghee out of the tin for cooking, he would scream out in anger, and draw my attention to the fact that its contents were diminishing much more rapidly than they should. When the dustman came to empty the refuse from the bin, he would go through it carefully before putting it out on the landing. One day he discovered some leftover scraps of food, and started yelling at me so loudly, that all the neighbours could hear. After this incident, he got into the habit of beating me whether he had a reason for it or not.

On one occasion he hit me all over with his shoe. My face and body became swollen and bruised. So I left the house and went to my uncle. But my uncle told me that all husbands beat their wives, and my uncle's wife added that her husband often beat her. I said my uncle was a respected Sheikh, well versed in the teachings of religion, and he, therefore, could not possibly be in the habit of beating his wife. She replied that it was precisely men well versed in their religion who beat their wives. The precepts of religion permitted such punishment. A virtuous woman was not supposed to complain about her husband. Her duty was perfect obedience.

I was at a loss what to answer. Before the servant girl had even started putting lunch on the table, my uncle took me back to my husband's house. When we arrived he had already eaten his lunch alone. Night fell, but he did not ask me whether I was hungry. He had his dinner alone and in silence, without addressing a single word to me. Next morning, I prepared breakfast and he sat down on his chair to eat, but avoided looking at me. When I sat down at the table, he looked up and started to stare fixedly at my plate. I was terribly hungry and felt a crying need to eat something, come what may. I put my hand in the plate and raised it to my mouth with a morsel of food. But no sooner had I done this than he jumped up shouting:

'Why did you come back from your uncle's house? Couldn't he bear to feed you for a few days? Now you will realize I'm the only person who can put up with you, and who is prepared to feed you. Why do you shy away from me then? Why do you turn your face away from mine? Am I ugly? Do I smell? Why do you keep at a distance whenever I come near to you?'

He leapt on me like a mad dog. The hole in his swelling was oozing drops of foul-smelling pus. I did not turn my face or my nose away this time. I surrendered my face to his face and my body to his body, passively, without any resistance, without a movement, as though life had been drained out of it, like a piece of dead wood or old neglected furniture left to stand where it is, or a pair of shoes forgotten under a chair.

One day he hit me with his heavy stick until the blood ran from my nose and ears. So I left, but this time I did not go to my uncle's house. I walked through the streets with swollen eyes, and a bruised face, but no one paid any attention to me. People were rushing around in buses and in cars, or on foot. It was as though they were blind, unable to see anything. The street was an endless expanse stretched out before my eyes like a sea. I was just a pebble thrown into it, battered by the waves, tossed here and there, rolling over and over to be abandoned somewhere on the shore. After some time I was worn out by walking, so I sat down to rest on an empty chair that I suddenly came upon placed upright on the pavement. A strong smell of coffee reached my nostrils. I realized my tongue was dry, and that I was hungry. When the waiter boy came up to me and asked me what I would like to drink, I begged him to bring me a glass of water.

He looked at me angrily, and said that the coffee-house was not for passers by. He added that the Sayeda Zeinab mausoleum was very close, and that there I could find all the water I needed. I raised my eyes to look at him. He stared at me, and then asked me what had caused all the bruises on my face. I tried to say something in reply, but the words would not come so I hid my face in my hands and wept. He hesitated for a moment, then left me, and came back after a while carrying a glass of water. But when I put the glass to my lips, the water stuck in my throat, as though I was choking, and trickled back out of my mouth. After some time the owner of the coffee-house came over to where I was sitting and asked me what my name was.

'Firdaus,' I said.

Then he added, 'What are all these bruises on your face? Has somebody hit you?'

Once more I tried to explain but my voice choked again. I was breathing with difficulty, and kept swallowing my tears. He said, 'Stay here and rest for a while. I will bring you a cup of hot tea. Are you hungry?'

All the time I kept my eyes fixed on the ground, and did not raise them to look at his face even once. His voice was low, with a slight hoarseness which reminded me of my father. After he had eaten his meal, and beaten my mother and calmed down, he would ask me,

'Are you hungry?'

For the first time in my life I suddenly felt my father had been a good man, that I missed him, and deep down inside had loved him without really knowing it. I heard the man say,

'Is your father alive?'

I answered, 'No, he's dead,' and for the first time wept at the thought that he had died. The man patted my shoulder and said,

'Everyone has to die, Firdaus,' and added, 'What about your mother. Is she alive?'

'No,' I replied.

He insisted 'Haven't you got any family? A brother, or an

uncle of some sort?'

I shook my head, repeating, 'No,' then quickly opened my small bag, adding, 'I have a secondary school certificate. Maybe I can find a job with my secondary, or with my primary school certificate. But if necessary I'm prepared to do anything, even the kind of work that requires no certificates.'

His name was Bayoumi. When I lifted my eyes and looked into his face, I felt no fear. His nose resembled that of my father. It was big and rounded, and he had the same dark complexion. His eyes were resigned and calm. They did not seem to me like the eyes of someone who would kill. His hands looked obedient, almost submissive, their movements quiet, relaxed. They did not impress me as the hands of someone who could be violent or cruel. He told me he lived in two rooms and that I could stay in one of them until I found work. On the way to his house he stopped in front of a fruit stall and said,

'Do you prefer oranges or tangerines?'

I tried to reply but my voice failed me. No one had asked me before whether I preferred oranges or tangerines. My father never bought us fruit. My uncle and my husband used to buy it without asking me what I preferred. As a matter of fact, I myself had never thought whether I preferred oranges to tangerines, or tangerines to oranges. I heard him ask me again,

'Do you like oranges or tangerines?'

'Tangerines,' I answered. But after he had bought them, I realized that I liked oranges better, but I was ashamed to say so, because the tangerines were cheaper.

Bayoumi had a small two-room flat in a narrow lane. It overlooked the fish market. I used to sweep and clean the rooms, buy fish from the market below us, or a rabbit, or meat and cook for him. He worked all day in the coffee-house without eating, and when he came back at the end of the day he would eat a heavy meal, and then go to sleep in his room. I used to sleep in the other room lying on the floor with a mattress under my body.

The first time I went home with him it was winter and the night was cold. He said to me,

'You take the bed, and I will sleep on the floor.'

But I refused. I lay down on the floor and started to fall asleep. But he came over to me, took hold of my arm, and took me to the bed. I moved by his side with bent head. I was so embarrassed, that I stumbled several times. Never in my life had anyone put me first before himself. My father used to occupy the oven room in winter, and leave me the coldest room in the house. My uncle had the bed to himself, while I slept on the wooden couch. Later on, when I married, my husband ate twice as much food as I did, yet his eyes never lifted themselves from my plate.

I stood for a moment near the bed and murmured: 'But I cannot sleep on the bed.'

I heard him say, 'I will not let you sleep on the floor.'

My head was still bent to the ground. He kept his hand clasped around my arm. I could see it was a big hand with long fingers like those of my uncle when he touched me, and now they were trembling in exactly the same way. And so I closed my eyes.

I felt the sudden touch of him, like a dream remembered from the distant past, or some memory that began with life. My body pulsed with an obscure pleasure, or with a pain that was not really pain but pleasure, with a pleasure I had never known before, had lived in another life that was not my life, or in another body that was not my body.

I ended up by sleeping in his bed throughout the winter and the following summer. He never raised a hand to strike me, and never looked at my plate while I was eating. When I cooked fish I used to give it all to him, and just take the head or the tail for myself. Or if it was rabbit I cooked, I gave him the whole rabbit and nibbled at the head. I always left the table without satisfying my hunger. On my way to market my eyes would follow the schoolgirls as they walked through the streets, and I would remember that at one time I had been one of them, and had obtained a secondary school certificate. And one day I stopped right in front of a group

48

of schoolgirls and stood there facing them. They eyed me up and down with disdain for there was a strong smell of fish arising from my clothes. I explained to them that I had been awarded a secondary school certificate. They started to make fun of me, and I heard one of them whisper into her friend's ear:

'She must be mad. Can't you see, she's talking to herself?'

But I was not talking to myself. I was just telling them that I had a secondary school certificate.

That night when Bayoumi came home, I said, 'I have a secondary school certificate, and I want to work.'

'Every day the coffee-house is crowded with youths, who are out of work, and all of them have university degrees,' he said.

'But I must work. I can't carry on like this.'

Without looking me in the face, he said, 'What do you mean, you can't carry on like this?

'I cannot continue to live in your house,' I stammered. 'I'm a woman, and you're a man, and people are talking. Besides, you promised I'd stay only until you found me a job.'

He retorted angrily, 'What can I do, get the heavens to intervene for you?'

'You're busy all day in the coffee-house, and you haven't even tried to find me a job. I'm going out now to look for one.'

I was speaking in low tones, and my eyes were fixed on the ground, but he jumped up and slapped me on the face, saying, 'How dare you raise your voice when you're speaking to me, you street walker, you low woman?'

His hand was big and strong, and it was the heaviest slap I had ever received on my face. My head swayed first to one side, then to the other. The walls and the floor seemed to shift violently. I held my head in my hands until they grew still again, then I looked upwards and our eyes met.

It was as though I was seeing the eyes that now confronted me for the first time. Two jet black surfaces that stared into my eyes, travelled with an infinitely slow movement over my face, and my neck, and then dropped downwards gradually over my breast, and my belly, to settle somewhere just below it, between my thighs. A cold shiver, like the shiver of death went through my body, and my hands dropped instinctively to cover the part on which his gaze was fixed, but his big strong hands moved quickly to jerk them away. The next moment he hit me with his fist in the belly so hard that I lost consciousness immediately.

He took to locking me in the flat before going out. I now slept on the floor in the other room. He would come back in the middle of the night, pull the cover away from me, slap my face, and then bear down on me with all his weight. I kept my eyes closed and abandoned my body. It lay there under him without movement, emptied of all desire, or pleasure, or even pain, feeling nothing. A dead body with no life in it at all, like a piece of wood, or an empty sock, or a shoe. Then one night his body seemed heavier than before, and his breath smelt different, so I opened my eyes. The face above me was not Bayoumi's.

'Who are you?' I said.

'Bayoumi,' he answered,

I insisted, 'You are not Bayoumi. Who are you?'

'What difference does it make? Bayoumi and I are one.' Then he asked, 'Do you feel pleasure?'

'What did you say?' I enquired.

'Do you feel pleasure?' he repeated.

I was afraid to say I felt nothing so I closed my eyes once more and said, 'Yes.'

He sank his teeth into the flesh of my shoulder and bit me several times in the breast, and then over my belly. While he was biting me, he kept on repeating:

'Slut, bitch.' Then he started insulting my mother in words I was not able to follow. Later on, when I tried to pronounce them, I was not able. But after that night I heard them often from Bayoumi, and from Bayoumi's friends. So I got used to their sound, and learnt to use them occasionally myself when I tried to open the door and found it locked. I would hammer on it and scream:

'Bayoumi, you son of a . . .' almost on the point of insulting his mother in the same way, but I held back the words on the tip of my tongue, realizing that this would be wrong. So I resorted to insulting his father instead of his mother.

One day a neighbour saw me through the lattice of the door as I stood there weeping. She asked me what was wrong, so I told her. She started crying with me and suggested that we call the police. But the word police frightened me. Instead, I asked her to bring a carpenter. After a while he came and forced the door open. I ran out of Bayoumi's house into the street. For the street had become the only safe place in which I could seek refuge, and into which I could escape with my whole being. As I ran, I looked back over my shoulder now and again to make sure that Bayoumi was not following me. And every time I found that his face was not visible anywhere, I leapt forwards as fast as I could run.

At the end of the day I found myself walking down a street without knowing where I was. It was a clean, paved thoroughfare, which ran along one bank of the Nile with tall trees on either side. The houses were surrounded by fences and gardens. The air which entered my lungs was pure and free of dust. I saw a stone bench facing the river. I sat down on it, and lifted my face to the refreshing breeze. I had barely closed my eyes in rest, when I heard a woman's voice asking:

'What is your name?'

I opened my eyes to find a woman seated next to me. She was wearing a green shawl, and her eyes were shadowed with green make-up. The black pupils in the centre of her eyes seemed to have turned green, a powerful dark green, like the trees on the bank of the Nile. The waters of the river reflected the green of the trees, and flowed by as green as her eyes. The sky over our heads was as blue as the bluest sky, but the colours mingled and everything around radiated this liquid green light which surrounded me, enveloped me completely, so that I felt myself gradually drowning in it.

It was strange, this sensation of drowning in dark green, in a dark green with a density of its own, a consistency of its own, like the feel of water in the sea, a sea in which I was sleeping, and dreaming, in which I was sinking as I slept and dreamt, in which I was gradually sinking without getting wet, gradually dropping without getting drowned. I felt myself lying on its bed at one moment, swallowed deep down inside, and a moment later carried gently upwards, floating higher and higher back to its surface, without moving an arm or a leg.

I felt my eyelids getting heavier as if I were about to fall asleep, but her voice echoed in my ears again. It was a smooth voice, its depths so soft that it sounded almost drowsy. It said,

'You are tired.'

I forced up my eyelids with an effort and said, 'Yes.'

The green in her eyes grew even more intense. 'What did the son of a dog do to you?' she asked.

I gave a start like someone who has suddenly been awakened from sleep. 'Whom do you mean?' I asked.

She wrapped the shawl around her shoulders more closely, yawned and continued in the same soft drowsy voice.

'Any one of them, it doesn't make any difference. They're all the same, all sons of dogs, running around under various names. Mahmoud, Hassanein, Fawzy, Sabri, Ibrahim, Awadain, Bayoumi.'

I interrupted her with a gasp. 'Bayoumi?!'

She laughed out loud. I glimpsed her small, white pointed teeth, with a gold tooth right in the middle.

'I know them all. Which one of them started it? Your father, your brother . . ., one of your uncles?'

This time my body gave a violent start which almost lifted it off the stone bench.

'My uncle,' I replied in a low voice.

She laughed again and tossed the green shawl backwards

over one shoulder.

'And what did Bayoumi do to you?' She was silent for a moment, and then added, 'You haven't told me your name. What's your name?'

'Firdaus. And you? Who are you?' I asked.

She stiffened her back and neck with a movement full of a strange pride. 'I am Sharifa Salah el Dine. Everyone knows me.'

On the way to her apartment I talked all the time, describing the things that had happened to me. We left the road which ran along the river and turned off into a small side street, and after a little while halted in front of a large apartment building. I trembled as I felt myself carried upwards by the lift. She took a key out of her bag, and the next moment I stepped into a spotless apartment with carpeted floors, and a spacious terrace overlooking the Nile. She took me to the bathroom, showed me how to turn the hot and cold water taps on and off, so I could have a bath, and gave me some of her clothes. They were soft clothes with a lovely smell of perfume, and her fingers too were soft as she combed my hair, and arranged the collar of my dress around the neck. Everything around me had this smooth, soft quality about it. I closed my eyes, and abandoned myself to the softness of things. I felt my body was now like that of a new-born baby, soft and smooth like everything else in the flat.

When I opened my eyes and looked into the mirror I realized that now I was being born again with a new body, smooth and tender as a rose petal. My clothes were no longer rough and dirty, but soft and clean. The house shone with cleanliness. Even the air was clean. I breathed deeply to fill my lungs with this pure air. I turned around and saw her. She was standing close by watching me, her eyes radiating a strong, green light, the colour of the trees, and the sky, and the waters of the Nile. I abandoned myself to her eyes, and put my arms around her, whispering:

'Who are you?'

And she replied, 'Your mother.'

'My mother died many years ago.'

'Then your sister.'

'I have neither sister, nor brother. They all died when they were small, like chicks.'

'Everybody has to die, Firdaus. I will die, and you will die. The important thing is how to live until you die.'

'How is it possible to live? Life is so hard.'

'You must be harder than life, Firdaus. Life is very hard. The only people who really live are those who are harder than life itself.'

'But you are not hard, Sharifa, so how do you manage to live?'

'I am hard, terribly hard, Firdaus.'

'No, you are gentle, and soft.'

'My skin is soft, but my heart is cruel, and my bite deadly.'

'Like a snake?'

'Yes, exactly like a snake. Life is a snake. They are the same, Firdaus. If the snake realizes you are not a snake, it will bite you. And if life knows you have no sting, it will devour you.'

I became a young novice in Sharifa's hands. She opened my eyes to life, to events in my past, in my childhood, which had remained hidden to my mind. She probed with a searching light revealing obscure areas of myself, unseen features of my face and body, making me become aware of them, understand them, see them for the first time.

I discovered I had black eyes, with a sparkle that attracted other eyes like a magnet, and that my nose was neither big, nor rounded, but full and smooth with the fullness of strong passion which could turn to lust. My body was slender, my thighs tense, alive with muscle, ready at any moment to grow even more taut. I realized that I had not hated my mother, nor loved my uncle, nor really known Bayoumi, or any other man who belonged to his gang.

Sharifa said to me one day, 'Neither Bayoumi, nor any of his cronies realized your worth, because you failed to value yourself highly enough. A man does not know a woman's value, Firdaus. She is the one who determines her value. The higher you price yourself, the more he will realize what you are really worth, and be prepared to pay with the means at his disposal. And if he has no means, he will steal from someone else to give you what you demand.'

I was seized with wonder and asked her, 'And am I really of any value, Sharifa?'

'You are beautiful and have culture.'

'Culture?' I said. 'All I have is a secondary school certificate.'

'You belittle yourself, Firdaus. I never got further than a primary school certificate.'

'And do you have a price?' I asked cautiously.

'Of course. Nobody can touch me without paying a very high price. You are younger than I am and more cultured, and nobody should be able to come near you without paying twice as much as what is paid to me.'

'But I cannot ask for anything from a man.'

'Don't ask for anything. That's not your affair. It's mine.'

Can the Nile, and the sky, and the trees change? I had changed, so why not the Nile and the colour of the trees? When I opened the window every morning I could see the Nile flow by, contemplate the green of the water, and the trees, the vivid green light in which everything seemed to bathe, feel the power of life, of my body, of the hot blood in my veins. My body filled with a warmth as soft as the touch of the silken clothes in which I dressed, or the silken bed in which I slept. My nose filled with the fragrance of roses wafted across the open spaces. I let myself sink in this feeling of warmth and softness, drown in the perfume of gentle roses, savour the comfort of the silken sheets as I stretched my legs, and of the smooth pillow under my head. I drank in the liquid softness through my nose, my mouth, my ears, through every pore in my body with a thirst which knew no end.

At night, moonbeams flowed over me, silky and white, like the fingers of the man who lay by my side. His nails too, were clean and white, not like Bayoumi's nails, which were black as the night, nor like my uncle's nails with their edge of dark earth on the underside. I would close my lids and let my body bathe in the silvery light, let the silken fingers touch my face and lips, move down to my neck and bury themselves between my breasts.

I would nurse them between my breasts for a while, leave them to slip down over my belly, and then below it to the place between my thighs. Deep inside my body I could feel a strange trembling. At first it was like pleasure, a pleasure akin to pain. It ended with pain, a pain which felt like pleasure. It belonged to a distant past, had been with me somehow right from the beginning. I had experienced it long ago, but forgotten it at the time. Yet it seemed to go back even further than my life, to some day before I was born, like a thing arising out of an ancient wound, in an organ which had ceased to be mine, on the body of a woman who was no longer me.

One day I asked Sharifa: 'Why don't I feel anything?'

'We work, Firdaus, we just work. Don't mix feeling with work.'

'But I want to feel, Sharifa,' I exclaimed.

'You will get nothing out of feeling except pain.'

'Is there no pleasure to be had, even the slightest pleasure?'

She burst out laughing. I could see her small white, pointed teeth, with the gold tooth in the middle. She went quiet all of a sudden and looked at me gravely, then said,

'Does it not give you pleasure to eat roast chicken and rice? Does it not give you pleasure to wear these soft, silky clothes? Do you not feel pleasure at living in this warm, clean house, with its windows overlooking the Nile? Does it not give you pleasure when you open the window every morning, and look out at the Nile, and the sky, and the trees? Isn't all this sufficient for you? Why do you ask for more?'

It was not out of greed that I was thinking of other things. One morning I had opened the window as usual, but the Nile was no longer there. I knew the Nile was in the same place, its waters stretched out before my eyes, but I could no longer see it, as though the human eye is incapable of seeing what is within its reach. The perfumes which I had all around me, under my nose, they too had disappeared. I was unable to detect their odour, as though my nose, just like my eyes, could no longer register the things which were there in front of it. The softness, the silk, the comfortable bed, all the things I knew were still there, no longer existed for me.

I never used to leave the house. In fact, I never even left the bedroom. Day and night I lay on the bed, crucified, and every hour a man would come in. There were so many of them. I did not understand where they could possibly have come from. For they were all married, all educated, all carrying swollen leather bags, and swollen leather wallets in their inner pockets. Their swollen heavy paunches hung down with too much food, and their sweat ran copiously, filling my nostrils with a foetid smell, like stagnant water, as though it had been held back in their bodies for a long time. I turned my face away, but they insisted on pulling it back, on burying my nose in the smell of their bodies. They dug their long nails into my flesh and I would close my lips tightly trying to stifle any expression of pain, to hold back a scream, but in spite of my efforts they would part and let out a low, muffled moan. Often the man would hear it and mutter stupidly in my ear,

'Do you feel good?'

In answer I would purse my lips and prepare to spit in his face, but he would start biting them with his teeth. I could feel his thick saliva between my lips and with a push of the tongue sent it back into his mouth.

Among all these men there was only one man who was not stupid, and did not ask me if I was feeling good. Instead he queried,

'Do you feel any pain?'

'Yes,' I said.

'What's your name?'

'Firdaus. And you?'

'I'm Fawzy.'

'How did you realize I was feeling pain?'

'Because I feel you.'

'You can feel me?' I exclaimed with amazement.

'Yes,' he said. 'What about you. Do you also feel me?'

'I don't feel anything.'

'Why?'

'I do not know. Sharifa told me work is work, and that feelings do not come in where work is concerned.'

He gave a short laugh and kissed me on the lips. 'Sharifa's fooling you, and making money out of you, while all you get out of it is the pain.'

I cried. He wiped my tears away and took me in his arms. I closed my eyes and he kissed me gently on the lids. I heard him whisper:

'Do you want to sleep?'

'Yes.'

'Then sleep in my arms.'

'But what about Sharifa?'

'Don't be afraid of Sharifa.'

'And you? Aren't you afraid of her?'

He gave another of his short laughs and said, 'She is the one who fears me.'

I was still asleep in my bed with my eyes closed when I heard soft voices from beyond the wall separating Sharifa's room from mine. I heard her speaking to a man whose voice sounded familiar.

'You're going to take her away from me?'

'I shall marry her, Sharifa.'

'Not you. You don't marry.'

'That's all over. Now I'm older and want a son.'

'So that he can inherit your wealth?'

'Don't be sarcastic at my expense, Sharifa. If I wanted I could have become a millionaire, but I am a man who lives for the pleasures of life. I earn money to spend it. I refuse to be a slave, either to money, or to love.'

'Do you love her, Fawzy?'

'Am I capable of love? You told me once that I had lost the ability to love.'

'You neither love, nor marry. All you want to do is to take her away from me, just as you took Camelia away before.'

'It was Camelia who came with me.'

'She fell in love with you, didn't she?'

'So women love me. Is that my fault?'

'Woe betide any woman that loves you, Fawzy.'

'That's if I'm not in love with her myself.'

'And can you love a woman?'

'Sometimes. It does happen.'

'Were you in love with me once?'

'Are you going to start harking back to that question again? I haven't got time to waste as you know, and I'm taking Firdaus with me.'

'You're not taking her.'

'I am taking her.'

'Are you threatening me, Fawzy? I'm not afraid of your threats any more. You can't get the police on to me. I have more friends and connections in the police than you have.'

'Am I a man who has recourse to the police? Only a weak man needs to do that. And do you think I am a weak man, Sharifa?'

'What do you mean?'

'You know what I mean.'

'You're going to beat me up, is that it?'

'It's a long time since I last hit you. It looks as though you're yearning for a good hiding.'

'If you hit me I will hit back, Fawzy.'

'That's fine. We'll see who's the stronger of the two.'

'If you so much as lay a finger on me I'll get Shawki on to you.'

'Who the hell is this Shawki of yours? Do you have another man? Are you in love with someone else? Do you dare?'

I was unable to hear Sharifa's reply through the wall.

Perhaps her voice was so low that it did not reach me. Or he may have covered her mouth with his hand before she could say anything more. For I heard what seemed to me the sound of a hand being clapped over a mouth, followed by another sound very much like that of someone's hand patting a face. Then came a series of muffled noises. I was unable to tell whether they were gentle slaps on the face, or violent kisses. But after a short while I heard Sharifa protesting:

'No, Fawzy, no!'

His voice sounded like an angry hiss. 'No. No what, you slut?'

The bed creaked under them, then once again I heard Sharifa's voice like a series of gasps followed by the same protesting tone.

'No, Fawzy. For the Prophet's sake. You must not, you must not!!'

Through the wall came his panting angry hiss again. 'What the hell, woman. Must not what, and Prophet what? Who's this Shawki. I'll cut his throat.'

The creaking grew louder under the weight of the two bodies, as they embraced each other, wrestled with one another, alternately closing in and separating in a continuous movement which soon mounted to a strangely rapid, almost mad frenzy, shaking the bed under them violently with the shudders of a wild animal short of breath. The floor seemed to shake and pant. Then it was the wall. Even the bed on which I was lying picked up the frenzied rhythm, and began to shake.

The violent shaking went to my head. It was as though I awakened suddenly to what was going on around me. I saw Fawzy's face take shape out of a mist, as if in a dream, and I heard his voice echoing in my ears again:

'Sharifa's fooling you. She's making money out of you.'

Then came Sharifa's voice as she said:

'If you hit me, Fawzy, I will hit back.'

I opened my eyes. My body was stretched out on the bed without a man beside me, and the room around was dark and empty. I walked on the tip of my toes to Sharifa's room, and

found her lying naked with Fawzy at her side. I tiptoed back
to my room, put on the first dress I could lay my hands on,
took my little bag, and hurried down the flights of stairs
into the street.

It was night, a pitch black night with no moon. A bitterly
cold, winter night, with the streets of the city completely
deserted, and with the windows and the doors of the houses
all firmly closed to prevent the slightest draught of air
from penetrating. There I was walking through the cold,
wearing a thin, almost transparent dress, and yet I did not
feel it. I was surrounded by darkness on all sides, with
nowhere to go, but I was no longer afraid. Nothing in the
streets was capable of scaring me any longer, and the coldest
wind could no longer bite into my body. Had my body
changed? Had I been transported into another woman's
body? And where had my own, my real body, gone?
    I started to examine the fingers of my hand. The fingers
were mine, they had not changed. Long slender fingers. One
of the men once said he had never seen fingers like these
before. He said they looked strong and clever. That they
possessed a language of their own. When he kissed them they
seemed to speak to him with a voice he could almost hear.
I laughed and brought my fingers close up to my ears, but
could hear nothing. I laughed again, and this time my laughter
echoed in my ears. I was taken aback to hear my own
laughter in the silent night. I looked around me cautiously,
fearing that someone might hear me laughing alone, and carry
me off to the Abbasseya Mental Hospital. At first I could see
nothing, but a moment later I glimpsed a policeman approaching in the dark. He came right up to me, caught me by the
arm, and said:
    'Where are you going?'

'I don't know.'

'Will you come with me?'

'Where to?'

'To my house.'

'No . . . I have no trust in men any more.'

I opened my small bag, and showed him my secondary school certificate. I told him I was looking for a job with my secondary, or even with my primary school certificate. That if I did not find something this way, I was prepared to do any work.

He said, 'I'll pay you. Don't think I want to have you for nothing. I am not like other policemen. How much do you want?'

'How much do I want? I don't know.'

'Don't play games with me, and don't try to haggle with me either, or I'll take you off to the police station.'

'Why. I haven't done anything.'

'You're a prostitute, and it's my duty to arrest you, and others of your kind. To clean up the country, and protect respectable families from the likes of you. But I don't want to use force. Perhaps we can agree quietly without a fuss. I'll give you a pound: a whole pound. What do you say to that?'

I tried to shake free of him, but he held on to my arm, and started to walk me away from where we were standing. He took me through one dark, narrow alley after another, then through a wooden door into a room, where he made me lie down on a bed. He took off his clothes. I closed my eyes as I felt the familiar weight bear down on me, the familiar movement of fingers with dirty black nails travelling over my body, the panting breath, the foul sticky sweat, the shaking of the bed, and the floor, and the walls, as though the world was turning round and round. I opened my eyes, dragged my body off the bed, put on my dress, and then leant my head, my tired head against the door for a moment before leaving. I heard his voice say from behind me:

'What are you waiting for? I have no money on me tonight. I'll give you money the next time.'

I walked away through the narrow streets. It was still night and the air was bitterly cold. Now rain had started to fall turning the dusty ground under my feet to mud. There were piles of rubbish in front of the houses, and the smell of rot seemed to envelop me on all sides, to overcome me, to drown me under it, and I kept walking faster, trying to escape, to get out of the narrow twisting streets and alleys on to a tarred road, any tarred road on which I could step without sinking my shoes in mud.

When I reached one of the main roads the rain was still pouring down over my head. I sought shelter at one of the bus stops, took a handkerchief out of my bag, and started to wipe my face, my hair, my eyes. A white light penetrated to my eyes, and at first I thought it was the white colour of my handkerchief, but when I took it away, the light continued to shine brightly in my eyes, like the headlamps of a bus. I thought it was dawn, and that the buses had already started. But it was not a bus. It was a car which had pulled up in front of me with its headlights full in my eyes. Then a man got out and circled quickly round the car, opened the door on my side, bowed slightly and then very politely said:

'Please do get in out of the rain.'

I was shivering with cold, and my light dress was clinging to my body, soaked in rain. My breasts were showing almost naked under my dress, the nipples standing out in two dark circles. As he helped me into the car, he pressed his arm against them.

It was warm inside his house, and he helped me out of my dress, took off my muddy shoes, and washed my body with warm water and soap. Then he carried me to the bed. I closed my eyes as I felt the weight press heavily down on my chest and belly, and the fingers move over my body. But the nails were clean and manicured, the panting breath had an odour of scent, and the sweat ran sticky, but fresh.

When I opened my eyes I was bathing in sunlight. I looked around unable to recognize where I was. There I was, lying in an elegant bedroom, with a stranger standing in front of me. I got up quickly and put on my dress and shoes. As I picked up my little bag and started to move towards the door, he stretched out his arm and slipped a ten pound note between my fingers. It was as if he had lifted a veil from my eyes, and I was seeing for the first time. The movement of my hand as I clasped the ten pound note solved the enigma in one swift, sweeping movement, tore away the shroud that covered up a truth I had in fact experienced when still a child, when for the first time my father gave me a piastre, a coin to hold in my hand, and be mine. My father had never given me money. I worked in the fields, and worked in the house, and together with my mother ate the scraps of food left over from my father. And on those days when there was no food left over from him, I went to bed without supper. On the *Eed El Kebir* I saw the children buy candy from a sweetshop. I went to my mother crying loudly 'Give me a piastre.'

She answered, 'I have no piastres. It's your father who has the piastres.'

So I went in search of my father and asked him for a piastre. He hit me on my hand and shouted, 'I have no piastres.'

But a moment later he called me back and said, 'I'll give you a piastre if Allah is bountiful to us and we manage to sell the buffalo before she dies.'

After that I saw him praying and exhorting Allah to delay the hour of her death. But the buffalo died before anyone could do anything. My father ceased his prayers and exhortations to Allah throughout the *Eed*, and whenever my mother said something to him he would jump at her and give her a beating. I refrained from asking him for a piastre but later, on the occasion of the *Eed El Sagheer* I noticed the sweets piled up in the shop, and said to my father,

'Give me a piastre.'

This time he said, 'Do you ask for a piastre, first thing in the morning? Go and clean under the animals and load the ass and take her to the fields. At the end of the day I shall give you a piastre.'

And in fact, when I returned from the fields at the end of that day, he gave me the piastre. It was the first piastre he had ever given me, the first piastre that was all mine, to put in the palm of my hand, and surround with my fingers, and squeeze. It was not my father's and not my mother's, but mine; mine to do with it what I wanted, to buy what I wanted, to eat with it whatever I desired, whether sweets, or *carob*, or molass sticks, or anything else I might choose.

The sun was shining brightly that day. I walked with a quick, energetic step, my right fist clenched tightly over something in my palm, something really valuable, not just a piastre this time, but a whole ten pound note. It was the first time I had held such a big note in my hand. As a matter of fact, it was the first time my fingers had even touched a note of that kind. The sudden contact sent a strange tautness through my body, an inner contraction as though something had jumped inside me and shaken my body with a violence which was almost painful. I felt as if something was pulsating out from a wound buried deep in my guts. When I stretched the muscles of my back, stood upright and breathed deeply it hurt. I could feel it rise up to my belly like a shiver, like blood beating strongly through the veins. The hot blood in my chest fose to my neck, swept through to my throat, to become a flow of warm rich saliva, bringing with it a savour of pleasure, so strong, so poignant that it was almost bitter.

I swallowed my saliva several times as I stood facing a glass partition behind which chickens were roasting on a brightly burning flame. My eyes gazed at them as they turned on the iron skewer over the leaping flames. I chose a table near a window so that it was covered in sunlight and ordered a fat, brown chicken. I sat down and started to eat it slowly, very slowly, chewing every morsel, keeping it in my mouth for a long moment before swallowing. My mouth was full, like that of a child stuffing itself with sweets, and the food had a strong, delicious taste, a strange powerful sweetness about it, like the sweetness of the molass stick bought with my first piastre. Yet that was not the first molass stick I had tasted, for my mother had bought me molass sticks before. But it was the first one I had chosen myself from amongst the other sweets in the shop, the first one bought with my own piastre.

The waiter bent over the table to place the other plates in front of me. He stretched out a hand with a plate full of food, but his eyes looked elsewhere, did not linger over my plate. The movement of his eyes as they avoided my plate cut like a knife through the veil which hung over my eyes, and I realized this was the first time in my life I was eating without being watched by two eyes gazing into my plate to see how much food I took. Ever since I was born those two eyes had always been there, wide open, staring, unflinching, following every morsel of food on my plate.

Was it possible that a mere piece of paper could make such a change? Why had I not realized this before? Was I really unaware of this throughout the years? No. Now that I thought about it I could see that I had known it for a very long time, right from the start, when I was born and opened my eyes to look at my father for the first time. All I could see of him was a fist, its fingers closed strongly over something in the palm of his hand. He never opened up his fingers, and even when he did, always kept something behind in his hand, something bright in colour, and circular in shape, something he used to handle gently with his big rough fingers or drop on a smooth stone so that it let out a ringing sound.

I was still sitting in the sun. The ten pound note lay in my bag, for I had not yet paid for my meal. I opened my bag to take it out. The waiter approached, bowed over the table with a movement of respectful humility and started to collect the plates. He kept his eyes away from my bag, looking all the while in another direction as though avoiding the ten pound note. I had seen this movement of the eyes before, this lowering of the lids, this almost imperceptible glance at my hand. It reminded me of my husband, Sheikh Mahmoud, as he kneeled in prayer, his eyes half-closed, of the glances he stole now and then at my plate; and of my uncle as he followed the lines in his book with peering eyes while his hand stole out from behind, searching for my thigh. The waiter was still standing upright by my side. His half-closed lids drooping over the eyes, his stealthy way of glancing aside were the same. I held the ten pound note in my hand, a and he watched it through the corner of one eye, while his other eye looked away as though shunning the forbidden parts of a woman's body. I was seized with a feeling of wonder. Could it be that the ten pound note I held in my hand was as illicit and forbidden as the thrill of sacrilegious pleasure?

I almost opened my mouth to ask the waiter, 'Who has decided that the ten pound note is to be considered forbidden?' But I kept my lips pressed tightly together for I had, in fact, known the answer all along, found it out many years ago, right from the moment when my father hit me over the hand when I first held it out for a coin. It was a lesson oft repeated, as time went by. My mother had once beaten me for losing a piastre in the market place, and returning home without it. My uncle was in the habit of giving me money, but warned me not to mention anything about it to my mother. My uncle's wife used to hide the piastres in her bodice whenever she heard me approaching before she had finished counting. My husband counted his piastres almost every day, but as soon as he saw me coming, he put them away. And Sharifa too, would count the pound notes, and stack them quickly in some secret recess the moment she heard my voice. And so, as the years went by, I began to look in the other direction every time I saw someone count his money, or even take a few coins out of his or her pocket. It was as though money was a shameful thing, made to be hidden, an object of sin which was forbidden to me and yet permissible for others, as though it had been made legitimate only for them. I was on the point of asking the waiter who it was that had decided all this, who it was that had decided for whom it was permissible, and to whom it should be forbidden. But I pressed my lips even more tightly together and held back the words. Instead I held out the ten pound note to him. He kept his head bent downwards, his eyes seemed to stray far away, as he put out his hand and took it from me.

From that day onwards I ceased to bend my head or to look

away. I walked through the streets with my head held high, and my eyes looking straight ahead. I looked people in the eyes, and if I saw someone count his money, I fixed it with an unwinking gaze. I continued to walk the streets. The sun was on my back. It flowed through me with its rays. The warmth of good food ran through my body with the blood in my veins. The rest of the ten pound note nestled safely in my pocket. My footsteps on the dark tarmac road struck the ground with force, with a new elation, like the elation of a child that has just pulled a toy to pieces and discovered the secret of how it works.

A man came up to me and whispered. I looked him straight in the eye and said 'No'. Another man came up to me and muttered something in a secretive voice which could barely be heard. I examined him carefully from head to toes and said, 'No'. He enquired: 'Why no?' I replied: 'Because there a are plenty of men and I want to choose with whom to go.'

So he said,'Well then, why not choose me?'

'Because your finger nails are dirty, and I like them to be clean.

A third man approached. He pronounced the secret word, the key to the riddle I had solved. I asked,

'How much will you pay?'

'Ten pounds.'

'No, twenty.'

'Your wishes are my orders,' and he paid me on the spot.

How many were the years of my life that went by before my body, and my self became really mine, to do with them as I wished? How many were the years of my life that were lost before I tore my body and my self away from the people who held me in their grasp since the very first day? Now I could decide on the food I wanted to eat, the house I pre- ferred to live in, refuse the man for whom I felt an aversion no matter what the reason, and choose the man I wished to have, even if it was only because he was clean and well manicured. A quarter of a century had passed, for I was twenty-five years old when I first started to have a clean apartment of my own, overlooking the main street, engage a cook who prepared the food I ordered, and employ someone to arrange for my appointments at the hours which suite suited me, and in accordance with the terms which I considered acceptable. My bank account kept mounting all the time. I now had free time in which I could relax, go for walks, or to the cinema, or the theatre, time to read the newspapers and to discuss politics with the few close friends I selected from the many who hovered around me seeking to strike up a friendship.

One of my friends was called Di'aa. He was a journalist, or a writer, or something of the sort. I preferred him to my other friends because he was a man of culture, and I had developed a liking for culture, ever since I had started to go to school and had learned to read, but especially during this last period, since I could now buy books. I had a large library in my apartment, and it was here that I spent most of my free time. On the walls I had hung some good paintings, and right in the middle was my secondary school certificate surrounded by an expensive frame. I never received anyone in the library. It was a very special room reserved for me alone. My bedroom was where I received my guests. The first time Di'aa came to my house, before I had time to lift the embroidered quilt which covered my bed, he said,

'Wait a moment, let's talk to one another for a while. I prefer talking to anything else.'

I was facing the bed with my back to him, so I did not see his expression when he pronounced these words. But his voice in my ear had a different tone, a tone I had never heard in the other men's voices.

I turned round so that I could see his face. I was not in the habit of turning round in order to look at the man's face. I would lift the embroidered quilt off the bed without looking at him, without even trying to glimpse something of his features. I used to keep my eyes tightly closed all the time and only open them when the weight pressing down on me had lifted from my body.

I turned round, raised my head, and looked straight into his face. I could see that his features, like his voice, had something about them that I had never come across before. His head seemed too big for his body, and his eyes looked small relative to his face. His skin was dark, but his eyes were not black, although I was not able to distinguish their exact colour in the dimmed electric light. His wide forehead started high up and swept down to a small nose. Below the nose his upper lip was shaven, and the thinning hair looked scanty on the overlarge head.

Since I stood there facing him without saying a word, he thought I had not heard him. He repeated:

'Let's talk a little. I prefer talking to anything else.'

'Nevertheless you will have to pay me like they all do. The time you can spend with me is fixed, and every minute counts as money.'

'You make me feel I'm in a clinic. Why don't you hang up a price list in the waiting room? Do you also have emergency visits?'

There was a note of irony in his voice, but I could not see why, so I said,

'Are you being sarcastic about my work, or about the medical profession?'

'Both,' he said.

'Are they similar to one another?'

'Yes,' he said, 'except that a doctor while carrying out his duties feels he's worthy of respect.'

'What about me?' I exclaimed.

'You are not respectable,' he replied, but before the words 'not respectable' had even reached my ears, my hands rose to cover them quickly, but they penetrated into my head like the sharp tip of a plunging dagger. He closed his lips tightly. A sudden deep silence enveloped the room, but the words continued to echo in my ears, took refuge in their innermost depths, buried themselves in my head, like some palpable material object, like a body as sharp as the edge of a knife which had cut its way through my ears, and the bones of my head to the brain inside.

My hands were still raised to cover my ears and shut out the sound of his voice. His voice was no longer audible to me, and when he spoke I could not see the movement of his lips, as though they remained invisible. The words seemed to emerge from between them, to escape of their own accord. I could almost see them as they traversed the space separating his lips from my ears, like tangible things with a well-defined surface, exactly like blobs of spit, as though he had aimed them at me from between his lips.

When he tried to brush his lips against mine, his words were still resonating in my mind. I pushed him away from me and said,

'My work is not worthy of respect. Why then do you join in it with me?'

He tried to take me by force, but I repelled his advances, then went to the door and opened it, and he immediately left.

But although Di'aa went out of my house, his words did not leave my ears with him that night. They had cut their way through to my mind in a moment of time which now belonged to the past. But no force on earth could turn back the hands of time one single moment. Before that moment my mind had been calm, tranquil, undisturbed. Every night I used to lay my head on the pillow and sleep deeply, right through the night until morning. But now my head vibrated with an incessant movement that kept on without respite, throughout the day, and throughout the night, like the ebb and flow of waves on a shore, seething and foaming and bubbling like boiling water. A sound like the roar of an angry sea went back and forth from my ears to the pillow, and from the pillow to my ears. In this storm I could no longer tell which was the rushing sound of the sea, and which was the blowing sound of the wind, for everything had become just a series of blows which followed one another like night and day, like my heartbeats racing in a row like a hammer in my head ringing out one phrase with every blow: 'not respectable', 'not respectable', hammering it out, blow after blow, into my bones, outside my bones, over my bed, on the floor, in the dining room, on the stairs, in the streets, on the walls. Wherever I went the strokes of the hammer beat down on my head, on my face, on my body, on my bones. Wherever I went the words clung to me cold and sticky like spit, like the spit of an insult echoing in the ear, like the spit of insolent eyes over my naked body, like the spit of all the degrading words I had heard ringing in my ears at one or other time, like the spit of all the brazen eyes that undressed me and examined my nakedness with a slow insolence, like the spit of courteous eyes that looked aside as I shed my clothes, hiding their contempt under a respectful guise.

One phrase, one small phrase composed of two words threw a glaring light on the whole of my life, and made me see it as it really was. The veil was torn from my eyes. I was opening them for the first time, seeing my life in a new way. I was not a respected woman. It was something I had not known before. It was as well that I had remained ignorant of the fact. I was able to eat well, and sleep deeply. Was there any way of uprooting this new knowledge from my mind? After all, it was only like some pain, cutting with the sharp edge of a knife through my head. In fact, it was not even a knife, but only a small phrase composed of two words, a small phrase which had penetrated like an arrow into my brain before I had the time to clap my hands over my ears and keep it out. Was there anything that could uproot it from my head the way they extract a bullet, or excise a tumour of the brain?

Nothing in the world seemed capable of making me the same woman I had been before I heard the two words pronounced by the man that night. From that moment onwards

I became another woman. My previous life was behind me. I did not want to go back to it at any price, no matter what torture and suffering I might have to go through, even if I were to know hunger and cold, and utter destitution. Come what may, I had to become a respectable woman, even if the price were to be my life. I was prepared to do anything to put a stop to the insults that my ears had grown used to hearing, to keep the brazen eyes from running all over my body.

I still had my secondary school certificate, my certificate of merit, and a sharp decisive mind determined to find respectable work. I still had two black eyes that looked people straight in the face and were ready to counter the shifty, leering glances thrown at me as I made my way through life. Every time there was an advertisement I applied for the job. I went to all the ministries, departments, and company offices where there might be a vacancy. And finally, by dint of these efforts, I at last found a job with one of the big industrial concerns.

Now I had a small office of my own, separated from the chairman's spacious room by a small door. Above the door protruded a red light, and near it was a bell. When the bell rang I would push open the door and enter his room. There he sat behind his desk, a man of about fifty, fat and bald, smoking all day. Some of his teeth were missing, and those that remained were stained yellow with black patches. He would look up from his papers with a cigarette dangling from his lips and say,

'Today I'm out for everybody except the really top people. Understood?'

And before I could ask him what he meant by 'the really top people' his head would bend over his papers once more, and almost disappear in the clouds of cigarette smoke.

After the day's work was over, I would pick up my little bag and go home. What I called home was not a house, or a flat, but merely a small room without a toilet. I rented it from an old woman who got up every morning at dawn to pray, then knocked at my door. My work did not start until eight o'clock in the morning, but I was always up at five, so that I would have the time to take my towel, and go down to join the queue of men and women standing in front of the bathroom. For my meagre salary did not permit me to live anywhere else than in this house, situated in a narrow back street with rows of small shops where plumbers and blacksmiths plied their trade. I had to wind my way through several narrow streets and walk up part of the main road before reaching the bus stop. When the bus came to a halt every one of the men and women at the stop would struggle to push his way in. I would join the throng of jostling, fighting bodies. But once inside it was as though I had stepped into an oven, where the packed bodies had fused into a single mass.

The building of the company where I worked had two doors: one for the more important higher level employees which remained unguarded, and another for the lesser officials which was guarded by one of the employees, very much like some kind of a doorkeeper. He used to sit behind a little desk with a big register in front of him. The employees signed in the register when they arrived in the morning or left after the day's work was over. I used to run down the long list for my name and sign opposite it. Then next to my name the man would write down the exact time, to the minute, of my arrival. When I left at the end of the day, he would register my departure time with the same precision.

But the higher officials would come and go as they pleased. They all rode in cars, big or small. I used to glimpse them sitting in their cars as I stood on one leg in the bus, hemmed in by a mass of bodies. One day, as I was running after the bus, trying to find a foothold on to which I could jump, one of them saw me. His look was that of a top executive to a minor official. I felt it land on my head, and then drop down to my body like cold water, the blood rushed to my head, and my foot tripped over something, so I came to a sudden stop. He drove up to where I stood and said,

'I can give you a lift.'

I looked into his eyes. They clearly said, 'You're a poor, miserable employee, unworthy of esteem, running after a bus to catch it. I'll take you in my car because your female body has aroused me. It is an honour for you to be desired by a respected official like myself. And who knows, maybe some day in the future, I can help you to get a rise before the others.'

When I said nothing, he thought I had not heard him. So he repeated: 'I can give you a lift.'

I quietly replied, 'The price of my body is much higher than the price that can be paid for it with a pay rise.'

His eyes widened with surprise. Maybe he was wondering how it was that I had read his thoughts so easily. I watched him as he drove off at high speed.

After I had spent three years in the company, I realized that as a prostitute I had been looked upon with more respect, and been valued more highly than all the female employees, myself included. In those days I lived in a house with a private toilet. I could enter it at any time, and lock the door on myself without anybody hurrying me. My body was never hemmed in by other bodies in the bus, nor was it a prey to male organs pressing up against it from in front and behind. Its price was not cheap, and could not be paid for by a mere rise in salary, an invitation to dinner, a drive along the Nile in somebody's car. Nor was it considered the price I was supposed to pay in order to gain my director's good will, or avoid the chairman's anger.

Throughout those three years not once did a top executive or higher official so much as touch me. I had no wish to humiliate my body at a low price, especially after I had become accustomed to being paid very highly for whatever services I rendered. I even refused invitations to lunch, or to a drive along the Nile. After a long day's work, I preferred to go home and sleep. I felt sorry for the other girls who were guileless enough to offer their bodies and their physical efforts every night in return for a meal, or a good yearly report, or just to ensure that they would not be treated unfairly, or discriminated against, or transferred. Every time one of the directors made me a proposition, I would say to him,

'It's not that I value my honour and my reputation more than the other girls, but my price is much higher than theirs.'

I came to realize that a female employee is more afraid of losing her job than a prostitute is of losing her life. An employee is scared of losing her job and becoming a prostitute because she does not understand that the prostitute's life is in fact better than hers. And so she pays the price of her illusory fears with her life, her health, her body, and her mind. She pays the highest price for things of the lowest value. I know knew that all of us were prostitutes who sold themselves at varying prices, and that an expensive prostitute was better than a cheap one. I also knew that if I lost my job, all I would lose with it was the miserable salary, the contempt I could read every day in the eyes of the higher level executives when they looked at the lesser female officials, the humiliating pressure of male bodies on mine when I rode in the bus, and the long morning queue in front of a perpetually overflowing toilet.

I was not too keen on keeping my job, and perhaps for that very reason the company authorities seemed to become more and more keen to keep me. I did not make any special effort to curry the favour of one or other of the higher officials. On the contrary, it was they who started vying with one another for my favours. And so the word went round that I was an honourable woman, and a highly respected official, in fact the most honourable, and the most highly considered of all the female officials in the company. It was also said that none of the men had succeeded in breaking my pride and that not a single high-ranking official had been able to make me bow my head, or lower my eyes to the ground.

But I liked my job despite everything. At work I met my women colleagues. I could talk to them and they could talk to me. My office was better than the room in which I lived.

There was no queue outside the office toilets, and nobody hurried me when I was inside. The grounds around the office building had a small garden in which I could sit for a while at the end of the day before going home. Sometimes night would fall and I would still be there, in no hurry to return to my dreary room, the dirty back streets and the foul smelling toilets.

One day as I sat there one of the employees saw me. For a moment he was scared by the sight of a dark mass, the size of a human body, crouched motionless in the dark of night. He called out from a distance:

'Who is it? Who is sitting there?'

I said in a sad voice, 'It's me, Firdaus.'

When he came nearer he recognized me, and seemed surprised to see me sitting there alone, for I was considered one of the best employees in the company, and the best employees were expected to leave immediately the day's work was over.

I said I was having a rest because I felt tired. He sat down next to me. His name was Ibrahim. He was a short, stocky man, with rather fuzzy black hair, and black eyes. I could see them in the night looking at me, and felt that they were able to see me despite the dark. Every time I moved my head away they followed me, held on fast refusing to let go. Even when I hid my eyes behind my hands they seemed to pierce through them to what was there behind. But after a while he took hold of my hands, gently pulled them away from my face, and said,

'Firdaus, I beg of you. Don't cry.'

'Let me cry,' I said.

'But I've never seen you cry before. What's happened?'

'Nothing . . . Nothing at all.'

'That's not possible. Something must have happened.'

'Nothing at all has happened,' I repeated.

He sounded surprised. 'Are you crying for nothing?'

'I do not know why I am crying. Nothing new had happened in my life.'

He remained seated by my side in silence. His black eyes wandered into the night, and the tears welled up in them for a moment with a glistening light. He tightened his lips and swallowed hard, and suddenly the light in his eyes went out. Then they started to shine again, but an instant later went dark, like tiny flames snuffed out in the night. He kept pressing his lips together and swallowing hard, but at last I saw two tears overflow from his eyes, and drop down on either side. He hid his face with one hand, pulled out a handkerchief with the other, and wiped his nose.

'Are you crying, Ibrahim?' I asked.

'No, Firdaus.'

He hid the handkerchief, swallowed with an effort and smiled at me.

The courtyard around us was plunged in a deep silence. There was not a sound to be heard and everything was motionless, suspended , without movement. The sky above was enveloped in darkness with not a ray of light from sun or moon. My face was turned towards his face, and my eyes looked into his eyes. I could see two rings of pure white surrounding two circles of intense black looking out at me. I continued to gaze into them. The white seemed to grow even whiter, and the black to become even blacker, as though light flowed through them from some unknown, mysterious source, neither on earth, nor in the heavens, for the earth was enveloped in the dark cloak of night, and the heavens had neither sun nor moon to light them up.

I held his eyes fast in mine. I reached out and took his hand in mine. The feel of our hands touching was strange, sudden. It made my body tremble with a deep, distant pleasure, older than the age of remembered life, deeper than the consciousness carried within me throughout. I could feel it somewhere in my being, like a part which had been born with me when I was born, but had not grown with me when I had grown. Or like something I had known before being born, and left behind.

At that moment a memory came back to me and my lips parted to express it in words, but my voice failed to emerge, as though no sooner did I remember than I had already forgotten it. My heart faltered, overcome by its frightened almost frenzied beating because of something I had just lost, or was on the point of losing for ever. My fingers grasped at his hand with such violence that no force in the world, no matter how great, could take it away from me.

After that night we only had to meet and my lips would part to say something. But no sooner did I remember it than it was already forgotten. My heart beat with fear, or with an emotion akin to fear. I wanted to reach out and take his hand, but he would enter the premises and leave them without noticing me, and if he looked at me it was in the same way that he looked at any other female employee.

At a big meeting for the workers I heard him speak about justice and the abolition of privileges enjoyed by management as compared to the workers. We applauded him enthusiastically and stood at the door for a long time to shake his hand. When my turn came I held his hand in mine, and his eyes in my eyes for a long moment. Sitting at my desk I would absent-mindedly jot down his name 'Ibrahim' on the wooden surface, or on the back of my hand, and no sooner did I glimpse him crossing the inner courtyard, than I would stand up as though getting ready to rush off and join him. But a moment later I would sit down again. My friend, Fatheya, caught me standing up and sitting down again like that several times. She came up to me and whispered into my ear:

'What's happened to you, Firdaus?'

And I would question in a musing voice, 'Has Ibrahim forgotten?'

'Forgotten what?' she would say.

'I don't know, Fatheya.'

'You're living in a dream world, my dear girl.'

'That's not true. That's not true, Fatheya. It happened.'

Then she would ask, 'What is it exactly that happened?'

I tried to tell her what had happened, but did not know how to describe it to her, or maybe I could not find anything to say, as if something had happened, but I had forgotten exactly what it was, or as if nothing had happened at all.

I would close my eyes, and try to bring back the scene. The two circles of deep black surrounded by two rings of intense white would gradually appear before my eyes. When I stared into them for some time, they would start to expand, rapidly becoming bigger and bigger, so that at a certain moment the black reached the size of the earth, and the white grew into a piercingly white mass, as big as the disc of the sun. My eyes would lose themselves in the black and the white until they could no longer perceive either of them. The images before my eyes grew confused. I could no longer distinguish between the faces of my mother and my father, of Wafeya and Fatheya, of Iqbal and Ibrahim. I opened my eyes wide in panic, like someone threatened with losing her sight. The outlines of Fatheya's face were still there, standing out against the dark colour of the earth, or the shining white of the sun.

'Do you love Ibrahim?' she asked.

'Not at all.'

'Why then do you tremble whenever you hear his name mentioned?'

'Me? Never! It has never happened. You always exaggerate, Fatheya.'

I heard her say, 'Ibrahim is a fine man, and a revolutionary.'

'I know. But I am no more than a minor employee. How could Ibrahim possibly fall in love with a poor girl like me?'

A revolutionary committee was set up in the company, with Ibrahim as its chairman. I joined the committee and started to work for it day and night, including holidays. It was voluntary work. I no longer worried about my wages. Waiting in the morning queue for the toilet no longer bothered me, and the pressure of bodies surrounding me no longer filled me with humiliation. One day Ibrahim saw me running after the bus, stopped his small car and called out to me. I got in next to him. A moment later I heard him say,

'I admire you, Firdaus. If we had just five people in the company with your zeal, energy and conviction, we could do almost anything in the world.'

I said nothing. I was pressing my little bag against my breast, trying to cover up the pounding of my heart, and to make my breathing return to normal. But after a while I realized that my breathing was still hectic. In an attempt to conceal the emotion I felt, I proffered an excuse which sounded rather lame:

'I'm still out of breath from chasing that bus.'

He must have realized what I was trying to do, for he just smiled without making any comment. After a while he asked me,

'Do you want to go straight home or shall we sit somewhere and talk?'

The question took me by surprise and I answered on the spur of the moment without thinking,

'I don't want to go home.' Then in order to cover up the slip I had made, added quickly, 'You must be tired after a long day's work. Perhaps you had better go straight home and rest.'

'Maybe it will do me more good to talk to you for a while. That's, of course if you are not tired yourself and would prefer to rest at home.'

Almost unaware of what I was saying, I replied, 'Rest! I have never known what it means to rest in my life.'

I felt his strong warm hand take hold of mine. I felt myself trembling all through. Even the roots of the hair on my body seemed to move.

He asked in a quiet voice, 'Firdaus. Do you remember the first time we met?'

'Yes.'

'Ever since that day I have been thinking about you.'

'And I, too, have been thinking about you.'

'I have been trying to hide my feelings, but it's no longer possible.'

'So have I.'

That day we talked about everything. I described my childhood, and what had happened to my life in the past, and he, too, spoke to me of his childhood years and the dreams he had for the future. The next day we met again and talked even more freely about everything. I even spoke to him about things I had hidden from myself, and refused to face. And he, in turn, was very frank with me, and hid nothing. On the third day he took me to his small house and I spent the night with him. We talked very quietly for a long time and when we had said all we had to say, we gave ourselves to one another in a warm embrace.

It was as though I held the whole world captive in my hands. It seemed to grow bigger, to expand, and the sun shone brighter than ever before. Everything around me floated in a radiant light, even the morning queue in front of the toilet. The eyes of the people riding in the buses no longer looked dull and jaundiced, but glowed and shone with a new light. When I looked into the mirror my eyes sparkled like diamonds. My body had become like a feather, and I could work all day without tiring, or feeling a need to sleep.

One morning a colleague of mine in the office stared at my face, and then exclaimed with a note of wonderment in her voice:

'What's going on, Firdaus?'

'Why?' I enquired.

'Your face is not the same.'

'What do you mean, not the same?'

'It's as though it's radiating some inner glow.'

'I'm in love.'

'In love?'

'Do you know what it is to love?' I asked.

'No,' she said sadly.

'You poor thing,' said I.

'You poor, deluded woman,' said she, 'do you believe there is any such thing as love?'

'Love has made me a different person. It has made the world beautiful.'

There was a deep note of sadness in her voice as she spoke. 'You're living an illusion. Do you believe the words of love they whisper in the ears of penniless women like us?'

'But he's a revolutionary. He's fighting for us and for all those who are deprived of a decent life.'

'You are really to be pitied. Do you think that what they say in their meetings is true?'

'That's enough,' I said angrily. 'You wear dark glasses over your eyes and then say you cannot see the sunshine.'

The sun was on my face. I gazed at the light and warmth around me, basking in it with wonder as I watched him cross the courtyard at the usual hour. His eyes sparkled in the sunshine with a strange new brilliance. They looked different to me, like the eyes of another man, and I felt estranged. I ran up to him but there was a group of employees gathered around him, men and women, shaking his hand and congratulating him. He did not see me in the crowd. I heard words that rung in my ears with a strange resonance:

'He got engaged to the chairman's daughter yesterday. He's a clever lad, and deserves whatever good fortune may come to him. He has a bright future to look forward to, and will rise quickly in the company.'

I put my hands over my ears to shut out the sound of their voices. I walked away from the happy throng around him, and left through the company gate, but did not go home.

I walked round and round in the streets. My eyes could see nothing, for the tears kept flowing from them, drying up now and then for a short while, only to start flowing once more. When night fell I was completely exhausted. All of a sudden my tears ceased to flow, as though something had closed up inside. Soon my face and neck became dry, but the front of my bodice was soaking wet. The cold night air penetrated to my body. I shivered and wound my arms around my chest to try and keep warm. I remembered his arms around me and shivered even more. I wept but the tears had dried once and for all. I heard a sound like that of a woman sobbing and realized that the voice I could hear was mine.

That night I went back to the company premises. I went into my office, collected my papers, put them in a small bag and then walked to the main door. Since I heard the news in the morning I had not seen Ibrahim again. I hesitated at the entrance for a moment and looked around slowly. My eyes wandered to the little garden in the back yard. I walked towards it and sat down. I kept looking around me all the time. Whenever I heard a sound coming from a distance, or sensed some movement or other, I strained my ears and my eyes. I saw a shape about the size of a human body moving near the entrance to the courtyard. I jumped to my feet. My heart beat wildly, the blood started pounding through my chest, up to my head. It seemed to me that the shape was moving towards me. I felt myself walking to meet it. My body was bathed in sweat. My head and the palms of my hands felt wet. A twinge of fear went through me as I moved across the dark courtyard. I called out in a voice so faint that it fell short of my ears:

'Ibrahim.'

But the silence remained as deep as before. I became even more frightened, for I could still see what looked like a human shape in the night. I called out again, this time in a loud voice that I could now hear:

'Who's there?'

It was as if the loud voice dispelled the dream like someone talking in his sleep is awakened by the sound of his own voice. The darkness lifted to reveal a brick wall which had been built in front of the entrance to the courtyard. It was a low wall, the height of an average man, built of bare bricks without any plaster. Although I had seen it before it seemed to have sprung up in front of my eyes at that very moment.

Before I went out through the gate, I looked around me

once more. My eyes swept the windows, the doors, and the walls, searching for something to open suddenly and reveal his eyes for a moment, or his hand waving the usual farewell. My eyes kept moving restlessly. At every moment I would lose all hope, only to regain it a moment later. My eyes would resume their frenzied search, and my breast would heave up and down more deeply. Before stepping out into the street I paused for a last moment, standing motionless in the dark. Even as I walked down the street I continued to turn round as though expecting something to happen, but the windows and doors remained as tightly shut as before.

I had never experienced suffering such as this, never felt a deeper pain. When I was selling my body to men the pain had been much less. It was imaginary, rather than real. As a prostitute I was not myself, my feelings did not arise from within me. They were not really mine. Nothing could really hurt me and make me suffer then the way I was suffering now. Never had I felt so humiliated as I felt this time. Perhaps as a prostitute I had known so deep a humiliation that nothing really counted. When the street becomes your life, you no longer expect anything, hope for anything. But I expected something from love. With love I began to imagine that I had become a human being. When I was a prostitute I never gave anything for nothing, but always took something in return. But in love I gave my body and my soul, my mind and all the effort I could muster, freely. I never asked for anything, gave everything I had, abandoned myself totally, dropped all my weapons, lowered all my defences, and bared my flesh. But when I was a prostitute I protected myself, fought back at every moment, was never off guard. To protect my deeper, inner self from men, I offered them only an outer shell. I kept my heart and soul, and let my body play its role, its passive, inert, unfeeling role. I learnt to resist by being passive, to keep myself whole by offering nothing, to live by withdrawing to a world of my own. In other words, I was telling the man he could have my body, he could have a dead body, but he would never be able to make me react, or tremble, or feel either pleasure or pain. I made no effort, expended no energy, gave no affection, provided no thought. I was therefore never tired or exhausted. But in love I gave all: my capabilities, my efforts, my feelings, my deepest emotions. Like a saint, I gave everything I had without ever counting the cost. I wanted nothing, nothing at all, except perhaps one thing. To be saved through love from it all. To find myself again, to recover the self I had lost. To become a human being who was not looked upon with scorn, or despised, but respected, and cherished and made to feel whole.

I was not destined to achieve what I had hoped for. For no matter how hard I tried, or what sacrifices I made like some dreamer sold to a cause, I still remained a poor insignificant employee. My virtue, like the virtue of all those who are poor, could never be considered a quality, or an asset, but rather looked upon as a kind of stupidity, or simple-mindedness, to be despised even more than depravity or vice.

The time had come for me to shed the last grain of virtue, the last drop of sanctity in my blood. Now I was aware of the reality, of the truth. Now I knew what I wanted. Now there was no room for illusions. A successful prostitute was better than a misled saint. All women are victims of deception. Men impose deception on women and punish them for being deceived, force them down to the lowest level and punish them for falling so low, bind them in marriage and then chastise them with menial service for life, or insults, or blows.

Now I realized that the least deluded of all women was the prostitute. That marriage was the system built on the most cruel suffering for women.

It was midnight and the streets were quiet. A gentle breeze was beckoning softly from the Nile. I walked along, enjoying the peace of the night. I no longer felt any pain. Everything around seemed to fill me with tranquillity. The gentle breeze caressing my face, the empty streets, and the rows of closed windows and doors, the feeling of being rejected by people and at the same time being able to reject them, the estrangement from everything, even the earth, and the sky and the trees. I was like a woman walking through an enchanted world to which she did not belong. She is free to do what she wants, and free not to do it. She experiences the rare pleasure of having no ties with anyone, of having broken with everything, of having cut all relations with the world around her, of being completely independent and living her independence completely, of enjoying freedom from any subjection to a man, to marriage, or to love; of being divorced from all limitations whether rooted in rules and laws in time or in the universe. If the first man who comes along does not want her, she will have the next, or the one after. No need to wait any longer for just one man. No need to be sad when he does not turn up, or to expect anything and suffer when one's hopes are razed to the ground. She no longer hopes for anything or desires anything. She no longer fears anything, for everything which can hurt her she has already undergone.

My arms opened wide to embrace the night, and my voice started to hum a song I vaguely remembered having heard before:

> I hope for nothing
> I want for nothing
> I fear nothing
> I am free.

A magnificent, long-bonneted car pulled up in front of me.

When the man looked out of the window I laughed. In the soft luxurious bed, I turned over from one side to the other, but neither made any effort, nor experienced any pleasure or pain. As I turned over in the bed a thought flashed through my mind. Revolutionary men with principles were not really different from the rest. They used their cleverness to get, in return for principles, what other men buy with their money. Revolution for them is like sex for us. Something to be abused. Something to be sold.

I met Ibrahim by accident four years after he married. He wanted to come with me to my flat. I had not yet got over my love for him, so I refused. I would not prostitute myself with him. But several years after that I gave in to his insistence, and agreed to let him come to my place. He was on the point of leaving without making any gesture to show that he intended to pay me.

I said, 'You've forgotten to pay me.'

He took a ten pound note out of his wallet with trembling fingers, and gave it to me.

'My rate is not less than twenty pounds,' I explained, then added, 'sometimes it is even more.'

His hand started to tremble again as he extracted another ten pound note from the wallet. I realized that he had not really been in love with me, but came to me every night only because he did not have to pay.

I became aware of the fact that I hated men, but for long years had hidden this secret carefully. The men I hated most of all were those who tried to give me advice, or told me that they wanted to rescue me from the life I was leading. I used to hate them more than the others because they thought they were better than I was and could help me change my life. They saw themselves in some kind of chivalrous role — a role they had failed to play under other circumstances. They wanted to feel noble and elevated by reminding me of the fact that I was low. They were saying to themselves:

'See how wonderful I am. I'm trying to lift her out of the mud before it's too late, that slut of a woman.'

I refused to give them a chance to play this role. None of them was there to rescue me when I was married to a man who beat me up and kicked me every day. And not one of them came to my help when my heart was broken because I had dared to fall in love. A woman's life is always miserable. A prostitute, however, is a little better off. I was able to convince myself that I had chosen this life of my own free will. The fact that I rejected their noble attempts to save me my insistence on remaining a prostitute, proved to me this was my choice and that I had some freedom, at least the freedom to live in a situation better than that of other women.

A prostitute always says yes, and then names her price. If she says no she ceases to be a prostitute. I was not a prostitute in the full sense of the word, so from time to time I said no. As a result my price kept going up. A man cannot stand being rejected by a woman, because deep down inside he feels a rejection of himself. No one can stand this double rejection. And so every time I said no, the man would insist. No matter how high I raised the price he could not stand being refused by a woman.

I became a very successful prostitute. I was paid the highest price, and even men of great importance competed for my favours. One day a very important personality from a foreign state heard about me. He arranged things in such a way that he could look me over without my noticing. Immediately after he sent for me, but I refused to go. I knew that successful politicians cannot bear to accept defeat in front of others, probably because they always carry defeat within themselves. A human being cannot stand up to a double defeat. That is the secret of their continuous attempt to rise to power. They draw a feeling of supremacy from their power over others. It makes them feel victorious rather than defeated. It hides how essentially hollow they are inside, despite the impression of greatness they try to spread around them, which is all they really care for.

My refusal made him even more intent on gaining a victory over me. Every day he would send me a man from the police, and each time this man would try a different approach. But I continued to refuse. Once he offered me money. On another occasion he threatened me with prison. On still a third, he explained to me that refusing a Head of State could be looked upon as an insult to a great man and lead to strained relations between the two countries. He added that if I really loved my country, if I was a patriot, I would go to him at once. So I told the man from the police that I knew nothing about patriotism, that my country had not only given me nothing, but had also taken away anything I might have had, including my honour and my dignity. I was surprised to see that the man from the police looked as though his moral pride was greatly shaken by what I had said. How could anyone be devoid of patriotic feeling? I felt like exploding with laughter at the ridiculous stance he was taking, the paradox he personified, his double moral standards. He wanted to take a prostitute to this important personality's bed, like any common pimp would do, and yet talk in dignified tones of patriotism and moral principles. But I realized that the man from the police was only obeying orders, and that any order issued to him was elevated to a sacred national duty. Whether he took me to prison, or to an important man's bed, it was just the same to him. In both cases, he was fulfilling a sacred national duty. Where national duty was concerned, a prostitute could be awarded the highest honours, and murder could become an act of heroism.

I refused to go to men of this sort. My body was my property alone, but the land of our country was theirs to own. On one occasion they put me in prison because I turned down one of these important men. So I hired a very big lawyer, for a very big sum of money. Shortly after, I was released from gaol without charges. The court decided I was

90

an honourable woman. Now I had learnt that honour required large sums of money to protect it, but that large sums of money could not be obtained without losing one's honour. An infernal circle whirling round and round, dragging me up and down with it.

Yet not for a single moment did I have any doubts about my own integrity and honour as a woman. I knew that my profession had been invented by men, and that men were in control of both our worlds, the one on earth, and the one in heaven. That men force women to sell their bodies at a price, and that the lowest paid body is that of a wife. All women are prostitutes of one kind or another. Because I was intelligent I preferred to be a free prostitute, rather than an enslaved wife. Every time I gave my body I charged the highest price. I could employ any number of servants to wash my clothes and clean my shoes, hire a lawyer no matter how expensive to defend my honour, pay a doctor for an abortion, buy a journalist to publish my picture and write something about me in the newspapers. Everybody has a price, and every profession is paid a salary. The more respectable the profession, the higher the salary, and a person's price goes up as he climbs the social ladder. One day, when I donated some money to a charitable association, the newspapers published pictures of me and sang my praises as the model of a citizen with a sense of civic responsibility. And so from then on, whenever I needed a dose of honour or fame, I had only to draw some money from the bank.

But male noses have an uncanny way of sniffing out money. And so one day a man came along and asked me to marry him. I refused. The imprint of my husband's shoe was still

there on my body. Then came another one looking for
love, but I refused him too. Deep down inside of me there
were still vestiges of the old pain.

I thought I had escaped from men, but the man who
came this time practised a well-known male profession. He
was a pimp. I thought I could buy him off with a sum of
money, the way I did with the police. But he refused the
money, and insisted on sharing in my earnings. He said,

'Every prostitute has a pimp to protect her from other
pimps, and from the police. That's what I'm going to do.'

'But I can protect myself,' I said.

'There isn't a woman on earth who can protect herself.'

'I don't want your protection.'

'You cannot do without protection, otherwise the profession exercised by husbands and pimps would die out.'

'I refuse your threats.'

'But I'm not threatening you. I'm just giving you a little
advice.'

'And if I don't accept your advice?'

'Then I may be obliged to threaten.'

'How do you propose to threaten me?'

'I have my own ways of doing things. Every craft has its
tools.'

I went to the police, only to discover that he had better
connections than I. Then I had recourse to legal proceedings.
I found out that the law punishes women like me, but turns
a blind eye to what men do.

And this man, this pimp whose name was Marzouk,
enjoyed a good laugh as he watched me from a distance,
striving in vain to find some way of protecting myself from
him. One day he saw me entering my house and followed me.
I tried to shut the door in his face, but he took out a knife,
threatened me with it, and forced his way in.

'What do you want of me?' I asked.

'I want to protect you from other men,' he replied.

'But no one else besides you is menacing me.'

'If it isn't me, it will be someone else. There are pimps
running around everywhere. If you want me to marry you,

I'm perfectly willing to do so.'

'I don't see the need for you to marry me as well. It's enough that you take what I earn. My body at least is mine.'

He went on like a successful businessman: 'I'm in business. My capital is women's bodies and I don't mix work and love together.'

'Do you know anything about love?'

'Is there anyone who does not know what love is? Haven't you fallen in love at one time or another?'

'I have.'

'And now?'

'It's over, there's nothing left. And you?'

'It hasn't died yet.'

'Poor thing. How miserable you must be.'

'I tried to get over it, but failed.'

'Is it a man or a woman? Pimps usually prefer men.'

'No, it's a woman.'

'Do you keep her?'

'I'm giving her everything. My money, my mind, my body, my being, my energy. Everything, and yet I feel that I do not satisfy her, that she's in love with another man.'

'You poor thing.'

'Everybody's the same when it comes to love.'

He looked straight into my eyes and said, 'You're living an illusion. I can see in your eyes how love has broken the spirit that used to shine.'

'Love makes the eyes sparkle, it does not kill their shine.'

'You poor thing. You've never really known what it is to be in love. I'm going to teach you.'

He tried to pull me to him, but I pushed him away and said,

'I don't mix work with love.'

'Who said this is love. It's just part of the job.'

'Impossible.'

'For me the word impossible does not exist.'

He wound his arms around me. I felt the familiar weight pressing down on my breast, but my body withdrew, turned in on itself away from me, like some passive, lifeless thing, refusing to surrender, undefeated. Its passivity was a form of resistance, a strange ability not to feel either pleasure or pain, not to let a single hair on my head, or on my body, be moved.

So he began to share in everything that I earned, in fact to confiscate the larger part for himself. But each time he tried to come near me, I pushed him away, repeating:

'It's impossible. It's no use trying.'

Then he'd beat me up. And each time I would hear the same phrase repeated as he struck me: 'The word does not exist for me.'

I discovered he was a dangerous pimp who controlled a number of prostitutes, and I was one of them. He had friends everywhere, in every profession, and on whom he spent his money generously. He had a doctor friend to whom he had recourse if one of his prostitutes became pregnant and needed an abortion, a friend in the police who protected him from raids, a friend in the courts who used his legal knowledge and position to keep him out of trouble and release any of the prostitutes who found herself in gaol, so that she was not held up from earning money for too long.

I realized I was not nearly as free as I had hitherto imagined myself to be. I was nothing but a body machine working day and night so that a number of men belonging to different professions could become immensely rich at my expense. I was no longer even mistress of the house for which I had paid with my efforts and sweat. One day I said to myself,

'I can't go on like this.'

I packed my papers in a small bag and got ready to leave, but suddenly he appeared, standing in front of me.

'Where are you going?' he asked.

'I'm going to look for work. I still have my secondary school certificate.'

'And who said that you are not working?'

'I want to choose the work I'm going to do.'

'Who says anyone in this whole wide world chooses the

work he wants to do?'

'I don't want to be anybody's slave.'

'And who says there is anyone who is not someone else's slave? There are only two categories of people, Firdaus, masters and slaves.'

'In that case I want to be one of the masters and not one of the slaves.'

'How can you be one of the masters? A woman on her own cannot be a master, let alone a woman who's a prostitute. Can't you see you're asking for the impossible?'

'The word impossible does not exist for me,' I said.

I tried to slip through the door, but he pushed me back and shut it. I looked him in the eye and said,

'I intend to leave.'

He stared back at me. I heard him mutter, 'You will never leave.'

I continued to look straight at him without blinking. I knew I hated him as only a woman can hate a man, as only a slave can hate his master. I saw from the expression in his eyes that he feared me as only a master can fear his slave, as only a man can fear a woman. But it lasted for only a second. Then the arrogant expression of the master, the aggressive look of the male who fears nothing returned. I caught hold of the latch of the door to open it, but he lifted his arm up in the air and slapped me. I raised my hand even higher than he had done, and brought it down violently on his face. The whites of his eyes went red. His hand started to reach for the knife he carried in his pocket, but my hand was quicker than his. I raised the knife and buried it deep in his neck, pulled it out of his neck and then thrust it deep into his chest, pulled it out of his chest and plunged it deep into his belly. I stuck the knife into almost every part of his body. I was astonished to find how easily my hand moved as I thrust the knife into his flesh, and pulled it out almost without effort. My surprise was all the greater since I had never done what I was doing before. A question flashed through my mind. Why was it that I had never stabbed a man before? I realized that I had been afraid, and that the fear had been within me all the time, until the fleeting moment when I read fear in his eyes.

I opened the door and walked down the stairs into the street.
My body was as light as a feather, as though its weight had
been nothing more than the accumulation of fear over the
years. The night was silent, the darkness filled me with wonder, as though light had only been one illusion after another
dropping like veils over my eyes. The Nile had something
almost magical about it. The air was fresh, invigorating. I
walked down the street, my head held high to the heavens,
with the pride of having destroyed all masks to reveal what
is hidden behind. My footsteps broke the silence with their
steady rhythmic beat on the pavement. They were neither
fast as though I was hurrying away from something in fear,
nor were they slow. They were the footsteps of a woman
who believed in herself, knew where she was going, and could
see her goal. They were the footsteps of a woman wearing
expensive leather shoes, with strong high heels, her feet
arched in a feminine curve, rising up to full rounded legs,
with a smooth, taut skin and not a single hair.

No one would have easily recognized me. I looked no
different from respectable, upper-class women. My hair had
been done by a stylist who catered only for the rich. My
lips were painted in the natural tone preferred by respectable
women because it neither completely hides, nor completely
exposes their lust. My eyes were pencilled in perfect lines
drawn to suggest a seductive appeal, or a provocative with-
drawal. I looked no different from the wife of an upper-
class government official occupying a high position of
authority. But my firm, confident steps resounding on the
pavement proved that I was nobody's wife.

I crossed by a number of men working in the police force,
but none of them realized who I was. Perhaps they thought

I was a princess, or a queen, or a goddess. For who else would hold her head so high as she walked? And who else's footsteps could resound in this way as they struck the ground? They watched me as I passed by, and I kept my head high like a challenge to their lascivious eyes. I moved along as calm as ice, my steps beating down with a steady unfaltering sound. For I knew that they stood there waiting for a woman like me to stumble, so that they could throw themselves on her like birds of prey.

At the corner of the street I spotted a luxurious car, with the head of a man protruding from the window, its tongue almost hanging out. He opened the door of the car and said,

'Come with me.'

I held back and said, 'No.'

'I will pay whatever you ask for.'

'No,' I repeated.

'Believe me, I will pay you anything you want.'

'You cannot pay my price, it's very high.'

'I can pay any price. I'm an Arab prince.'

'And I am a princess.'

'I'll pay a thousand.'

'No.'

'Two thousand, then.'

I looked deep into his eyes. I could tell he was a prince or from the ruling family, for there was a lurking fear in their depths.

'Three thousand,' I said.

'I accept.'

In the soft luxurious bed, I closed my eyes, and let my body slip away from me. It was still young and vigorous, strong enough to retreat, powerful enough to resist. I felt his body bearing down on my breast, heavy with long untold years of his life, swollen with stagnant sweat. A body full of flesh from years of eating beyond his needs, beyond his greed. With every movement he kept repeating the same stupid question:

'Do you feel pleasure?'

And I would close my eyes and say, 'Yes.'

Each time he rejoiced like a happy fool, and repeated his question with a gasping breath and each time I gave the same answer: 'Yes.'

With the passing moments his foolishness grew, and with it his assurance that my repeated affirmations of pleasure were true. Every time I said 'yes' he beamed at me like an idiot, and an instant later I could feel the weight of his body bear down on me, more heavily than before. I could stand no more, and just when he was on the point of repeating the same stupid question again, I snapped out angrily,

'No!'

When he held out his hand with the money, I was still wildly angry with him. I snatched the notes from his hand and tore them up into little pieces with a pent-up fury.

The feel of the notes under my fingers was the same as that of the first piastre ever held between them. The movement of my hands as I tore the money to pieces, tore off the veil, the last, remaining veil from before my eyes, to reveal the whole enigma which had puzzled me throughout, the true enigma of my life. I rediscovered the truth I had already discovered many years before when my father held out his hand to me with the first piastre he had ever given me. I returned to the money in my hand and with a redoubled fury tore the remaining bank notes into shreds. It was as though I was destroying all the money I had ever held, my father's piastre, my uncle's piastre, all the piastres I had ever known, and at the same time destroying all the men I had ever known, one after the other in a row: my uncle, my husband, my father, Marzouk and Bayoumi, Di'aa, Ibrahim, and tearing them all to pieces one after the other, ridding myself of them once and for all, removing every trace their piastres had left on my fingers, tearing away the very flesh of my fingers to leave nothing but bone, ensuring that not a single vestige of these men would remain at all.

His eyes opened wide in amazement as he watched me tear up the whole sheaf of bank notes. I heard him say:

'You are verily a princess. How did I not believe you right from the start?'

'I'm not a princess,' I said angrily.

'At first I thought you were a prostitute.'

'I am not a prostitute. But right from my early days my father, my uncle, my husband, all of them, taught me to grow up as a prostitute.'

The prince laughed as he eyed me again and then said, 'You are not telling the truth. From your face, I can see you are the daughter of a king.'

'My father was no different from a king except for one thing.'

'And what is that?'

'He never taught me to kill. He left me to learn it alone as I went through life.'

'Did life teach you to kill?'

'Of course it did.'

'And have you killed anybody yet?'

'Yes, I have.'

He stared at me for a brief moment, laughed and then said, 'I can't believe that someone like you can kill.'

'Why not?'

'Because you are too gentle.'

'And who said that to kill does not require gentleness?'

He looked into my eyes again, laughed, and said, 'I cannot believe that you are capable of killing anything, even a mosquito.'

'I might not kill a mosquito, but I can kill a man.'

He stared at me once more, but this time only very quickly, then said, 'I do not believe it.'

'How can I convince you that what I say is true?'

'I do not really know how you can do that.'

So I lifted my hand high up above my head and landed it violently on his face.

'Now you can believe that I have slapped you. Burying a knife in your neck is just as easy and requires exactly the same movement.'

This time, when he looked at me, his eyes were full of fear.

I said, 'Perhaps now you will believe that I am perfectly

capable of killing you, for you are no better than an insect, and all you do is to spend the thousands you take from your starving people on prostitutes.'

Before I had time to raise my hand high up in the air once more, he screamed in panic like a woman in trouble. He did not stop screaming until the police arrived on the scene.

He said to the police, 'Don't let her go. She's a criminal, a killer.'

And they asked me, 'Is what he says true?'

'I am a killer, but I've committed no crime. Like you, I kill only criminals.'

'But he is a prince, and a hero. He's not a criminal.'

'For me the feats of kings and princes are no more than crimes, for I do not see things the way you do.'

'You are a criminal,' they said, 'and your mother is a criminal.'

'My mother was not a criminal. No woman can be a criminal. To be a criminal one must be a man.'

'Now look here, what is this that you are saying?'

'I am saying that you are criminals, all of you: the fathers, the uncles, the husbands, the pimps, the lawyers, the doctors, the journalists, and all men of all professions.'

They said, 'You are a savage and dangerous woman.'

'I am speaking the truth. And truth is savage and dangerous.'

They put steel handcuffs around my wrists, and led me off to prison. In prison they kept me in a room where the windows and the doors were always shut. I knew why they were so afraid of me. I was the only woman who had torn the mask away, and exposed the face of their ugly reality. They condemned me to death not because I had killed a man — there are thousands of people being killed every day — but because they are afraid to let me live. They know that as long as I am alive they will not be safe, that I shall kill them. My life means their death. My death means their life. They want to live. And life for them means more crime, more plunder, unlimited booty. I have triumphed over both life and death because I no longer desire to live, nor do I any longer fear to die. I want nothing. I hope for nothing. I fear nothing. Therefore I am free. For during life it is our wants, our hopes, our fears that enslave us. The freedom I enjoy fills them with anger. They would like to discover that there is after all something which I desire, or fear, or hope for. Then they know they can enslave me once more. Some time ago one of them came to me and said:

'There's hope for your release if you send an appeal to the President asking him to pardon you for the crime you committed.'

'But I don't want to be released,' I said, 'and I want no pardon for my crime. For what you call my crime was no crime.'

'You killed a man.'

'If I go out once again to the life which is yours I will never stop killing. So what is the use of my sending an appeal to the President to be pardoned?'

'You criminal. You deserve to die.'

'Everybody has to die. I prefer to die for a crime I have committed rather than to die for one of the crimes which you have committed.'

Now I am waiting for them. After a little while they will come to take me away. Tomorrow morning I shall no longer be here. I will be in a place which no one knows. This journey to an unknown destination, to a place unknown to all those who live on this earth, be they king or prince, or ruler, fills me with pride. All my life I was looking for something that would fill me with pride, something that would make me hold my head high, higher than the heads of everyone else, especially kings, princes and rulers. Every time I picked up a newspaper with the picture of one of them in it, I would spit on it. I knew I was only spitting on a piece of newspaper, which I might need to spread on the shelves of my kitchen, yet each time I used to spit, and leave the spit to dry on its own. Anyone who saw me spitting at the picture might think that I knew the man whose face I was spitting at personally. But in fact I did not know him. For after all, I'm only a lone woman. And one woman, no matter who she might be, cannot possibly know all the men who have their pictures published in the newspapers. Yes, no matter who she might be. I was no more than a successful prostitute, and no matter how successful a prostitute is, she cannot get to know all men. But with each of the men I ever knew, I was always overcome by a strong desire to lift my arm high up over my head and bring my hand smashing down on his face. Yet because I was afraid I was never able to lift my hand. Fear made me see this movement as being something very difficult to carry out. I did not know how to get rid of this fear, until the moment when I raised my hand for the first time. The movement of my hand upwards and then downwards destroyed my fear. I realized that it was an easy movement to execute, much easier than I ever thought it could be. Now my hand was no longer incapable of lifting itself high up in the air to land with violence on one of their faces. The movement of my hand had become very easy, and everything in my hand could be moved with a natural ease, even if it were a sharp knife which I thrust into a chest and then withdrew. It would penetrate in and come out with the natural ease of air entering the lungs and then flowing out. I am speaking the truth now without any difficulty. For the truth is always easy and simple. And in its simplicity lies a savage power. I only arrived at the savage, primitive truths of life after years of struggle. For it is only very rarely that people can arrive at the simple, but awesome and powerful truths of life after only a few years. And to have arrived at the truth means that one no longer fears death. For death and truth are similar in that they both require a great courage if one wishes to face them. And truth is like death in that it kills. When I killed I did it with truth not with a knife. That is why they are afraid and in a hurry to execute me. They do not fear my knife. It is my truth which frightens them. This fearful truth gives me great strength. It protects me from fearing death, or life, or hunger, or nakedness, or destruction. It is this fearful truth which prevents me from fearing the brutality of rulers and policemen.

I spit with ease on their lying faces and words, on their lying newspapers.

3

Firdaus' voice suddenly fell silent, like a voice in a dream. I moved my body like someone moving in sleep. What lay under me was not a bed, but something solid like the ground, and cold like the ground, yet with a coldness which did not reach my body. It was the cold of the sea in a dream. I swam through its waters. I was naked and knew not how to swim. But I neither felt its cold, nor drowned in its waters. Her voice was now silent, but its echo remained in my ears, like a faint distant sound. Like the voices one hears in a dream. They seem to come from afar although they arise from close by, or seem to be nearby although they come from afar. We do not know in fact from where they arise. From above or below. To our left or our right. We might even think they come from the depths of the earth, drop from the rooftops or fall from the heavens. Or they might even flow from all directions, like air moving in space reaches our ears. But this was not air flowing into my ears. The woman sitting on the ground in front of me was a real woman. The voice filling my ears with its sound, echoing in the cell where the window and the door were tightly closed, was a real voice. And I was certainly awake. For suddenly the door was thrown open, revealing several armed policemen. They surrounded her in a circle, and I heard one of them say:

'Let's go . . . Your time has come.'

I saw her walk out with them. I never saw her again. But her voice continued to echo in my ears, vibrating in my head, in the cell, in the prison, in the streets, in the whole world, shaking everything, spreading fear wherever it went, the fear of the truth which kills, the power of truth, as savage, and as simple, and as awesome as death, yet as simple and as gentle as the child that has not yet learnt to lie.

And because the world was full of lies, she had to pay the price.

I got into my little car, my eyes on the ground. Inside of me was a feeling of shame. I felt ashamed of myself, of my life, of my fears, and my lies. The streets were full of people bustling around, of newspapers hanging on wooden stalls, their headlines crying out. At every step, wherever I went, I could see the lies, could follow hypocrisy bustling around. I rammed my foot down on the accelerator as though in a hurry to run over the world, to stamp it all out. But the next moment I quickly lifted my foot and braked hard, and the car came to a halt.

And at that moment I realized that Firdaus had more courage than I.

Nawal El Saadawi

'The leading spokeswoman on the status
of women in the Arab World'
Guardian

Nawal El Saadawi – Egyptian novelist, doctor and militant writer on Arab women's problems and their struggle for liberation – was born in the village of Kafr Tahla. Refusing to accept the limitations imposed by both religious and colonial oppression on most women of rural origin, she qualified as a doctor in 1955 and rose to become Egypt's Director of Public Health. Since she began to write over 25 years ago, her books have concentrated on women. In 1972, her first work of non-fiction, *Women and Sex*, evoked the antagonism of highly placed political and theological authorities, and the Ministry of Health was pressurised into dismissing her. Under similar pressures she lost her post as Chief Editor of a health journal and as Assistant General Secretary in the Medical Association in Egypt. From 1973 to 1976 she worked on researching women and neurosis in the Ain Shams University's Faculty of Medicine; and from 1979 to 1980 she was the United Nations Advisor for the Women's Programme in Africa (ECA) and Middle East (ECWA). Later in 1980, as a culmination of the long war she had fought for Egyptian women's social and intellectual freedom – an activity that had closed all avenues of official jobs to her – she was imprisoned under the Sadat regime. She has since devoted her time to being a writer, journalist and worldwide speaker on women's issues.

The Hidden Face of Eve

This is a personal and often disturbing account of growing up into womanhood in the Islamic world. The author ranges over a host of topics – from sexual aggression against female children and the circumcision of young girls, to prostitution, sexual relationships, marriage and divorce. She relates women's position in the Middle East to the struggles between the left and right in Islam, and shows how the political priorities of Western and Third World women differ.

Nawal El Saadawi – doctor, writer and militant advocate of Arab women's rights – was born in Kafr Tahla village on the banks of the Nile. She was Egypt's Director of Public Health, until summarily dismissed as a consequence of her political activities. Undeterred by this, the banning of her books, and a period of imprisonment under Sadat, she continues to write about Arab women's problems and their struggle for liberation.

'Nawal El Saadawi ... speaks directly on behalf of many women in the Third World and the daily struggles they face'
West Africa

God Dies by the Nile

Zakeya hoes the stony fields on the banks of the Nile, each day as relentless and unchanging as the last. But when her two pretty young nieces fall prey to the lust of the local Mayor, a crude and petty tyrant, his cheating schemes provoke Zakeya into a startling act of revenge.

Written with all the sustained, brutal insistence of *Woman at Point Zero*, this tale of tragedy, deception and lust is also a moving political allegory.

The Circling Song

Hamida and Hamido are twins, grown from a single embryo inside one womb. Violently parted, they search the city in the darkening circles of a dream, only to find, lose and find each other, each time as if it were the first. Their journey – terrifying and exact – leads to an unbroken cycle of corruption and brutality.

With a precise and hypnotic intensity, Nawal El Saadawi pursues the conflicts of sex, class, gender and military violence deep into the psyche. *The Circling Song* is her most original novel.

Searching

Fouada meets Farid, her lover, every Tuesday in a restaurant overlooking the Nile. But this week their familiar table is deserted. She calls his home, but the shrilling of the telephone echoes in an empty room. Farid has disappeared.

As she searches for him, Fouada becomes tormented by questions. She is a trained research chemist, but works in a dead-end ministry job. Convinced that she has something significant to give to the world, she cannot find it. What is it? Why does she search?

Searching expresses the poignancy of loss and doubt with the hypnotic intensity of a remembered dream.